DREAMLAND

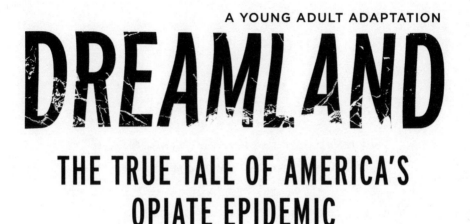

A YOUNG ADULT ADAPTATION

DREAMLAND

THE TRUE TALE OF AMERICA'S OPIATE EPIDEMIC

SAM QUINONES

BLOOMSBURY

NEW YORK   LONDON   OXFORD   NEW DELHI   SYDNEY

BLOOMSBURY YA
Bloomsbury Publishing Inc., part of Bloomsbury Publishing Plc
1385 Broadway, New York, NY 10018

BLOOMSBURY and the Diana logo are trademarks of Bloomsbury Publishing Plc

First published in the United States of America in July 2019 by Bloomsbury YA

No responsibility for loss caused to any individual or organization acting on or refraining from action as a result
of the material in this publication can be accepted by Bloomsbury or the author.

Bloomsbury Publishing Plc does not have any control over, or responsibility for, any third-party websites referred
to or in this book. All internet addresses given in this book were correct at the time of going to press. The author
and publisher regret any inconvenience caused if addresses have changed or sites have ceased to exist, but can accept
no responsibility for any such changes.

Bloomsbury books may be purchased for business or promotional use. For information on bulk purchases
please contact Macmillan Corporate and Premium Sales Department at specialmarkets@macmillan.com

Library of Congress Cataloging-in-Publication Data
Names: Quinones, Sam, author.
Title: Dreamland / by Sam Quinones.
Other titles: Dream land
Description: YA edition. | New York : Bloomsbury Children's Books, [2019]
Identifiers: LCCN 2018045397 (print) | LCCN 2018059709 (e-book)
ISBN 978-1-5476-0131-8 (hardcover) • ISBN 978-1-5476-0141-7 (e-book)
Subjects: LCSH: Drug traffic—Mexico—Juvenile literature. | Drug addiction—United States—Juvenile literature. |
Heroin abuse—United States—Juvenile literature. | Oxycodone—United States—Juvenile literature. |
Narcotics—United States—Juvenile literature. | American Dream.
Classification: LCC HV5840.M4 Q56 2019 (print) | LCC HV5840.M4 (e-book)| DDC 362.29/30973—dc23
LC record available at https://lccn.loc.gov/2018045397

Book design by John Candell
Typeset by Westchester Publishing Services
Printed and bound in the U.S.A. by Berryville Graphics Inc., Berryville, Virginia
2 4 6 8 10 9 7 5 3 1

All papers used by Bloomsbury Publishing Plc are natural, recyclable products made from wood grown in well-managed
forests. The manufacturing processes conform to the environmental regulations of the country of origin.

To find out more about our authors and books visit www.bloomsbury.com and sign up for our newsletters.

To my girls

CONTENTS

INTRODUCTION

On the east side of Columbus, Ohio, where Myles and Matt Schoonover grew up, lots of kids smoked weed and drank. But that was about it, especially at their private, suburban Christian high school.

Myles, the older by three years, partied as a teen but could also bear down and focus. Matt had attention deficit hyperactivity disorder, and schoolwork was harder for him. He started smoking pot and drinking somewhere around his junior year in high school.

Their parents, Paul and Ellen, were never sure when Matt started abusing pain pills. But by the time Matt joined Myles at a private Christian university in Tennessee in 2009, the younger brother was already getting high on them.

Matt, six feet six and burly, was a caring fellow with a soft side. "I love you, mommy," he wrote once to his mother, after his grandmother had been hospitalized for some time. "All this stuff with grandma has made me realize you really don't know how long you have on this earth. You're the best mom I could ask for."

Yet the pills seemed to keep him in a fog. Myles once had to take him to a post office so he could mail their mother a birthday card, as Matt seemed otherwise incapable of finding the place.

In 2010, Matt returned home to live with his parents while Myles went to graduate school. At home, Matt dressed neatly and worked full-time at catering companies. Unbeknownst to his parents, he had become a functional addict, using opiate prescription painkillers, Percocet above all. From there, he moved to OxyContin, a powerful pill made by Purdue Pharma.

In early 2012, his parents found out. They were worried but rationalized that a doctor had prescribed the pills. They weren't some street drug that you could die from, or so they believed. They took him to a doctor, who prescribed a weeklong home detoxification, using blood pressure and sleep medicine to calm the symptoms of opiate withdrawal.

Matt relapsed a short time later. At some point, he switched from pricy street OxyContin to the cheap black tar heroin that had saturated Columbus, brought in by young Mexican men from a small state on Mexico's Pacific coast called Nayarit.

In April 2012, Matt tearfully admitted his heroin problem to his parents. Stunned, they got him into a treatment center.

Myles hadn't spoken to his brother for some time when he called home one day.

"He's in drug rehab," said his mother.

"What? For what?"

Ellen paused, not knowing how to say it. "Matt is addicted to heroin."

Myles burst into tears.

Matt Schoonover came home from three weeks of rehab on May 10,

2012, and with that, his parents felt the nightmare was over. The next day, they bought him a new battery for his car and a new cell phone.

He set off to a Narcotics Anonymous meeting, then a golf date with friends. He was supposed to call his father after the NA meeting.

His parents waited all day for the call. That night, a policeman knocked on their door.

Matt was twenty-one when he overdosed on black tar heroin. More than eight hundred people attended his funeral.

In the months after Matt died, Paul and Ellen Schoonover were struck by what they didn't know. First, how could medicine lead to heroin and death? And what was black tar heroin? People who lived in tents under overpasses used heroin. Matt grew up in the best neighborhoods, attended a Christian private school and a prominent church. He'd admitted his addiction, sought help, and received the best residential drug treatment in Columbus. Why wasn't that enough?

Across the country, thousands of young people like Matt Schoonover were dying. Kids were dying in the Rust Belt of Ohio and the Bible Belt of Tennessee, as well as in the best country club enclaves of Charlotte, North Carolina. They were dying in California, Indiana, Utah, and New Mexico, and in Oregon and Minnesota and Oklahoma and Alabama.

Drug overdoses were killing more Americans every year than car accidents were. Most of the fatal overdoses were from opiates: prescription painkillers or heroin.

From those prescription pills, heroin had entered the mainstream. The new addicts were high school football players and cheerleaders. Kids got hooked in college and died there. Some of these addicts were from rough corners of rural Appalachia. But many more lived in communities where the driveways were clean, the cars were new, and the shopping centers attracted congregations of Starbucks, Home Depot, CVS, and Applebee's. They were the daughters of preachers, the sons of cops and doctors, the children of contractors and teachers and business owners and bankers.

And almost everyone was white.

Children of the most privileged group in the wealthiest country in the world were getting hooked and dying in almost epidemic numbers from substances meant to, of all things, numb pain.

I grew consumed by this story. It was about the United States and Mexico, about addiction and marketing, about wealth and poverty, about happiness and how to achieve it. It took me through the history of pain and a revolution in US medicine. I followed the tale through a small town of sugarcane farmers in Nayarit, Mexico, and a town of equal size in the Rust Belt of southern Ohio. I met cops and addicts, professors and doctors, public health nurses and pharmacists.

And I met parents—parents whose children were still alive but had shape-shifted into lying, thieving slaves to addiction. They went broke paying for rehab. They prayed that the child they'd known would reemerge. They were shell-shocked and unprepared for the sudden nightmare opiate abuse had wreaked and how deeply it mangled their lives.

And parents like Paul and Ellen Schoonover, who were still anguished and bewildered a year after Matt's death.

"I kept trying to figure out what just happened. Why did our lives become devastated?" Paul Schoonover said to me when we first met at his insurance agency in Columbus. "How could this have happened?"

Here's how.

PART I
The Pills

PORTSMOUTH, OHIO

In this hardworking industrial area in the Ohio River valley, people swore by Dr. David Procter.

He heard them and believed them when they said they were in pain. He understood when they needed a doctor's diagnosis to qualify for workers' compensation or disability. They may or may not have been legitimately hurt or disabled, but Procter processed workers' paperwork fast so that the payments would arrive quickly.

At the Southern Hills Hospital in Portsmouth, Ohio, he ran through his rounds—literally ran. He was at high speed, animated. He had a folksy style, talkative and easygoing, with a little bit of evangelist in him.

"His patients loved him because he had the ability to figure out what that person believed or needed or wanted," said Lisa Roberts, who was a hospital nurse at the time. "He was brilliant in that way, to forensically identify vulnerable people and figure out what they needed or believed. He would tell them they had all these things wrong with them."

A father of two sons, whose family lived in nearby Kentucky, he was also flashy in a way that was foreign to the Ohio River valley. He wore diamond rings and fur jackets. He drove a Porsche.

Procter, a Canadian, had come to the area in the late 1970s to join another doctor. Within a couple of years, they had split and that doctor passed away. In 1979, Procter set up his own clinic on the south side of the Ohio River, in tiny South Shore, Kentucky, just a short drive from Portsmouth. He took over a beige metal-framed building and called it Plaza Healthcare.

When he arrived, the region's best years had passed. Once, the area had boomed with a giant steel plant, several shoe factories, and the nation's largest shoelace maker. Portsmouth had been a bustling town of forty-two thousand, with two bowling alleys, a few department stores, and a movie theater downtown.

In the summer, everyone had gathered at Dreamland, a private swimming pool the size of a football field where people came from all over the county to swim, sun, and socialize.

Over decades, generations of the town grew up at the edge of its crystal-blue water. Toddlers played in the shallow end. In the middle were two concrete platforms from which older kids sunned themselves, then dove back in. On one side of the pool was an immense lawn where families set their towels. On the opposite side were locker rooms and a restaurant. Later, there were picnic areas and playgrounds, softball and football fields, basketball courts, and a video arcade.

For many years, Dreamland's manager, Chuck Lorentz, a Portsmouth High School coach and strict disciplinarian, walked the grounds with a yardstick, making sure teenagers minded his "three-foot rule" and stayed that far apart. He wasn't that successful. It seems half the town got their first kiss at the pool.

The endless summers started to lose their charm in the 1970s. Portsmouth and surrounding communities began to slump in response to global competition and cheap labor in other countries. Shoe factories closed and nothing moved in to replace them.

Detroit Steel departed in 1980. Thousands of jobs went with it. Other plants followed. A Walmart came in, but that hardly filled the need for good jobs.

Families fled to Columbus or Cincinnati or Nashville for work. Portsmouth's population fell to twenty thousand. Unsellable houses were rented out or stood empty after landlords moved away.

Remaining behind was a thin slice of educated people, who ran the schools or the hospitals. About the only new folks who came to Portsmouth then were merchants of the poor economy: check-cashing places and rent-to-own stores. Pawnshops and scrap metal yards opened.

And David Procter began to expand.

In the mid-1980s, the medical world wrestled with how to use the new opiates that pharmaceutical companies were developing to treat pain. David Procter was an early and aggressive adopter. At Plaza Healthcare, which took cash payments only, he prescribed these powerful pain relievers for neck, leg, and lower back pain and sports injuries.

He combined them with anxiety relievers called benzodiazepines, of which Valium and Xanax, Procter's favorites, are the best known. In this declining area, people had anxiety and they had pain, and anything that relieved pain was welcome. But opiates and benzos together also led quickly to addiction.

The Kentucky Board of Medical Licensure investigated Procter's practices in the late 1980s. True, he prescribed opiates aggressively. But he also discontinued them and urged his chronic-pain patients to exercise or try physical therapy. The board found no regulations were violated, but he was put on probation.

Portsmouth's troubles continued. The Dreamland pool declined and finally closed in 1993. It stood untouched for two years before developers filled it in and built an O'Reilly Auto Parts and cellphone store with a massive asphalt parking lot. Walmart became the spot to socialize.

By then, Procter was prescribing a lot of diet pills and stimulants, even to those who weren't overweight. A modest underground industry evolved in and around Portsmouth of scamming prescriptions for diet pills from willing doctors like Procter, then selling the pills on the street for a profit. His Plaza Healthcare clinic boomed.

In 1996, Procter took a liking to a brand-new, even more powerful painkiller. It was called OxyContin, and he told patients he was getting good results with it.

Kathy Newman, who had been a cheerleader at Portsmouth High School, had just graduated when she broke ribs in a car accident. She was hurting and the emergency room in town was wary of prescribing more than ibuprofen for pain. Her friends encouraged her to go see David Procter. He'll give you something that works, they promised.

At the clinic, Kathy walked into a madhouse. People were standing in the aisles, tense with anticipation. After three hours, she finally saw the doctor. Procter prescribed her 5 mg of Vicodin, a mix of an opiate called hydrocodone and acetaminophen, the pain-relieving ingredient in Tylenol. He also spent a half hour telling her that she would probably have back and hip pain for the rest of her life and would need this prescription forever.

Newman remembered being "scared to death" by the thought that she would have pain forever.

When she went back for a new prescription after a month, saying she was still in pain, he upped the dose. Within three months, she was prescribed 20 mg of OxyContin. Those prescriptions led to a fourteen-year addiction that left her zoned out for years.

Another patient was Randy, a guard at a nearby state prison who had suffered deep bruises to his back in a fight with an inmate.

Procter handled the paperwork so Randy could take off six months from work to recover, charging him two hundred dollars cash. He also prescribed OxyContin—40 mg, twice a day, for thirty days.

"Looking back on it, [the injury] was nothing that warranted that harsh of a drug," Randy recalled. "But at the time, you're thinking this is great because I don't feel my back."

When Randy finished the prescription, he figured he was better. But soon he was gripped by what he thought was the worst flu of his life. He ached, couldn't get out of bed, had diarrhea, and was throwing up. A friend suggested he might be going through withdrawal.

Then it hit him: You've got to go back.

Randy returned to Procter every month, paying two hundred dollars cash for a three-minute visit and an Oxy prescription. Procter's waiting room overflowed. People fought over space in line. Only a handful of patients were there for injuries. The rest were faking pain to get prescriptions, with the doctor's cooperation.

"You're seeing people who you know are probably going to be locked up in one of your cellblocks," Randy said. "It really humbles you."

Though he trusted Procter, he said, "After a while you realize this isn't right but there really isn't anything you can do about it. You're stuck. You're addicted." Before long, he found street dealers he could go to if he ran out during the month.

He returned to his prison job. But by then fully addicted to the pills, he began arriving late and making excuses. Desperate, he got into treatment. Three and a half years after going to David Procter the first time, he kicked his addiction.

For the Ohio River valley and America, it was just beginning.

OXYCONTIN

OxyContin is a simple pill. It contains only one drug: oxycodone, a painkiller. On a molecular level, oxycodone is similar to heroin.

Both come from the opium poppy, a plant with a story almost as old as man.

Mesopotamians grew the poppy at the Tigris and Euphrates. The Assyrians figured out how to slice open the plant's golf-ball-sized bulb and drain the goo inside that contains opium.

The ancient Egyptians first produced opium as a drug. (Thebaine, one of the organic chemicals in opium, is named for Thebes, the Egyptian city that was the first great center of opium-poppy production.)

Early civilizations saw opium as an antidote to the burdens of life—to sorrow and to pain—and as an effective sleep inducer. They also knew it as lethally poisonous and intensely habit-forming. But its benefits made the risks easy to overlook.

In the early 1800s, a German pharmacist's apprentice named Friedrich Sertürner isolated the sleep-inducing element in opium and named it morphine, for Morpheus, the Greek god of sleep and dreams. Morphine was more potent than simple opium and killed more pain.

What gives the morphine molecule its immense power, said Andy Coop, former chair of the Pharmaceutical Sciences Department at the University of Maryland in Baltimore, is that it evolved somehow to fit, key in lock, into the receptors that all mammals, especially humans, have in their brains and spines. These receptors—designed to create pleasure sensations when they receive endorphins the body naturally produces—are especially welcoming to the morphine molecule. The receptor combines with endorphins to give us those glowing feelings at, say, the feel of a furry puppy. But the morphine molecule can overwhelm the receptor, creating a far more intense euphoria than anything we come by internally. It also produces drowsiness, vicious constipation, and an end to physical pain.

For this reason, no plant has been studied more for its medicinal properties. From opium, humans have derived codeine, hydrocodone, oxymorphone, and heroin, as well as almost two hundred other drugs. (That list also includes compounds used to block opiates during an overdose and treat opiate-related addictions.)

Aspirin has a limit to the amount of pain it can calm. But the more morphine you take, Coop said, the more pain is dulled. Further, as bodies grow accustomed to the drug, people may need higher doses to calm the pain.

Morphine also can exact a mighty vengeance when an abuser dares to stop using it. In withdrawal from the drug, an addict leaves narcotized numbness and returns to life and to feeling. Humans who attempt to withdraw from the morphine molecule are tormented first with excruciating pain that lasts for days. If an addict was always constipated and nodding off, his withdrawals will bring ferocious diarrhea and a week of sleeplessness.

The drug has allowed for modern surgery, saving and improving too many lives to count. Most people will actually use it safely. Yet, it has also stunted and ended too many lives to count with addiction and overdose. Recent studies have found that up to thirty of every one hundred users will abuse opiates, and up to twelve of every one hundred will become addicted. Like no other particle on earth, the morphine molecule seems to possess both heaven and hell.

In 1916, German scientists first synthesized oxycodone from the opiate derivative thebaine. It came to the United States a couple of decades later, but it wasn't widely used for years.

In fact, opiate-based medicines in general were little used for much of the twentieth century. Doctors for decades were trained to see them as addictive and dangerous. They were even willing to let cancer patients agonize and dying patients suffer rather than prescribe those drugs.

That began to change in 1980, when Jan Stjernsward, a Swedish cancer doctor, was named chief of the cancer program for the World Health Organization. Stjernsward worked with other doctors and experts to develop the radical idea that they could treat terminally ill patients with morphine and other opiates. The result was what became known as the WHO Ladder, a practice of using increasingly powerful drugs if pain did not subside. Those drugs might include opiates combined with acetaminophen, like the hydrocodone-acetaminophen mix in Vicodin and Lortab or the oxycodone-acetaminophen combination in Percocet. Morphine was deemed "an essential drug" in cancer pain relief.

Then the WHO went further, asserting that freedom from pain is an essential human right.

At the time, the pharmaceutical company that would become known as Purdue Pharma was selling mostly antiseptics, a laxative, and an earwax remover. A subsidiary had previously developed the Continus formula for releasing a drug over time. It had only been used, however, for a timed-release asthma medicine.

With demand for morphine treatment climbing, Purdue put the two together in 1984 and produced its first pain-management drug, MS Contin. MS Contin sent morphine into a patient's bloodstream continuously—hence Contin—over several hours. To be long lasting, it came in extra-large doses of morphine: 15, 30, 60, 100, and 200 mg. Purdue marketed this heavy-duty pain relief for cancer patients and people just out of surgery.

Over time, doctors began to grow more comfortable prescribing opiates for surgery and disease and then more. More and more, they began to offer it for persistent pain, such as chronic sports injuries, arthritic knees, and headaches.

The increasing availability of powerful painkillers coincided with dramatic changes in American healthcare. Healthcare costs started to climb in the 1980s and 1990s, and health-insurance companies began to push back. For years, clinics like the Center for Pain Relief at the University of Washington medical school treated chronic pain with a combination of therapies, including prescriptions, physical and occupational therapy, and psychologists and social workers.

"We were trying to teach [patients] that they were the ones who controlled whether they were well or not well," said the center's former director Dr. John Loeser. "The patient has to do the work."

The center's program took three weeks and required patients to regularly do certain exercises and pay attention to diet. It was hard work that was designed to make patients healthier in the long run.

Not surprisingly, people who were in constant pain wanted quick fixes. "There is a philosophy among many patients—'I'm entitled to be free of pain,'" said Loeser.

Every pain can't be eliminated, however. "People are entitled to health care," he said, and pain management should be part of health care. "But they are not entitled to pain relief."

All those different treatments cost money. Insurance companies, too, began to push for quicker, cheaper fixes. They balked at paying for treatment that wasn't strictly medical, like physical, occupational, and psychological therapy. With smaller reimbursements, many pain clinics began to shut their doors.

Insurance companies also were squeezing regular doctors, reducing the services they paid for and negotiating lower fees. Chronic pain patients took more time for doctors to diagnose and treat, not less. But doctors had to see more patients and spend less time with each of them just to stay even.

"The way you're reimbursed in a day, if you actually take the time to treat somebody's pain, you'd be out of business," one longtime family doctor said.

As the time spent with patients fell, providers found that the new comfort with opiates gave them an option. As every doctor knows, nothing cuts short a patient visit like a prescription pad.

Attitudes changed rapidly. By the 1990s, a revolution in medical thought and practice was under way. The American Pain Society, an organization of scientists and doctors, advanced the idea that a patient's pain counteracted the euphoric effect of the drugs. So the risk of addiction was low when opiates were used to treat pain.

Doctors were urged to address the country's pain epidemic by prescribing these drugs. Interns and residents were taught that these drugs were now not addictive and that doctors thus had a mission, a duty, to use them. In some hospitals, doctors were told they could be sued if they did not treat pain aggressively.

To protect doctors in the event that patients became addicted, a number of states passed so-called intractable pain regulations. These laws exempted doctors from criminal prosecution if they prescribed opiates in the practice of responsible health care.

In 1996, Dr. James Campbell, the American Pain Society's president, proposed a new standard. "If pain were assessed with the same zeal as other vital signs are, it would have a much better chance of being treated properly," he said in a speech. "We need to train doctors and nurses to treat pain as a vital sign." The society trademarked the slogan "Pain: The Fifth Vital Sign," putting discomfort alongside a patient's pulse, blood pressure, body temperature, and respiration.

Other major organizations adopted the concept, including the government's Veterans Health Administration. The California legislature required hospitals and nursing homes to screen for pain along with the other vital signs.

Of course, pain is subjective, unlike other vital signs, but new tools were developed to address that. Two women from Tulsa, Oklahoma—nurse Donna Wong and child therapist Connie Baker—devised a much-used way of assessing pain in children. They asked them to point to one of six faces, ranging from a smiley face to a tearful, grimacing face. Adults are asked to quantify their pain according to a scale—numbered from 0 to 10, with 10 being worst.

From all this, the idea took hold that America was undertreating pain. Tens of millions of people, surveys reported, were in pain that wasn't being treated. Pain's undertreatment was viewed as unnecessary, for medicine now had tools to treat it.

And in 1996, a new tool was added: Purdue introduced OxyContin, 40 and 80 mg doses of oxycodone wrapped in a timed-release formula that slowly sends the drug into the body over several hours.

From the start, Purdue promoted OxyContin far beyond MS Contin's cancer and postsurgical patients. It positioned OxyContin as the opiate of choice in the WHO Ladder of pain management. The company aimed to convince doctors to aggressively treat noncancer pain and prescribe OxyContin for moderate pain lasting more than a few days, including for bad backs, tooth extraction, and headaches; as well as football, hockey, and dirt-bike injuries; broken bones; and, of course, after surgery. This was a vast new market for an opiate painkiller. US back-pain patients alone numbered some thirty-five million people; the total number of cancer patients was seven million.

Before OxyContin, pain patients spent most of their day thinking about pain, or the pills they needed every two to four hours to keep it at bay. Clock watching, it was called.

The long relief that the new drug promised remade the medical options for everyone. Doctors could help a patient in terrible distress and do it during a short appointment. For patients, two OxyContin pills a day would restore their lives—or so it seemed.

ADDICTION

OxyContin, no doubt, helped many Americans for whom life would otherwise be torture. But there was another major factor behind its early success: Purdue and others promoted it as less addictive than other opiates.

In theory, OxyContin parceled out oxycodone in a regulated way that did not create the intense highs and lows that caused addiction. This was an exciting possibility.

"It was the drug-delivery device that changed, not the drug, and with that the whole mentality, 'Well, now that we have this drug, we can treat pain.' Really extraordinary," said Dr. Kathleen Foley of New York's Memorial Sloan Kettering Cancer Center in an oral history interview the year OxyContin was released.

In late 1995, the US Food and Drug Administration approved OxyContin for 10, 20, and 40 mg pills. Later, it added 80 and 160 mg pills. Despite the high doses of oxycodone loaded into each pill, the

FDA bought the idea that by creating fewer surges of euphoria and depression, OxyContin would be less addictive—the Holy Grail of opiate pain relief.

FDA examiner Dr. Curtis Wright, supervisor of the agency's team that examined Purdue's application, thought OxyContin might actually possess addictive side effects. He thought the only real benefit was that it reduced the number of pills a patient had to take every day. Wright later left the FDA to work for Purdue.

The FDA also approved a unique warning label for OxyContin. It allowed Purdue to claim that OxyContin had a lower potential for abuse than other oxycodone products because its timed-release formula allowed for a delay in absorbing the drug.

Purdue set about promoting OxyContin as a virtually risk-free solution to patients' problems. The company urged doctors to believe that Oxy was the drug to "start with and stay with" because the oxycodone was released slowly over many hours.

Phillip Prior, a family physician at a local hospital in Chillicothe, Ohio, an hour north of Portsmouth, recalled Purdue salesmen coming through his hospital six times in 1997 alone. The salesmen would provide doctors an elaborate lunch of steak, salad, and dessert. They had slides and graphics that presented the startling idea that the company's new timed-release drug, OxyContin, was virtually nonaddictive.

Less than 1 percent of patients ever grew addicted, they said in their presentations. (The statistic was based on sparse data that had appeared years earlier in a medical journal, but no one ever questioned the source.)

The claim surprised Prior. In medical school in the early 1980s, "I was trained that [opiates] were dangerous, addictive and only effective for a short period of time," Prior said. He remembered a study that concluded that daily usage of 30 mg of oxycodone was enough to cause withdrawal.

But their pitch "was a very effective presentation," Prior said. "It really did make you doubt your feelings about what you'd been taught in medical school."

Purdue offered OxyContin coupons to physicians, who could in turn give them to patients for a one-time free prescription at a participating pharmacy. (By the time Purdue discontinued the program, thirty-four thousand coupons had been redeemed.)

The salesmen gave doctors OxyContin fishing hats, stuffed toys, coffee mugs, golf balls, and pens with a chart converting a patient's dose in other pills to OxyContin. They passed out *Swing Is Alive* CDs, which urged listeners to "Swing in the Right Direction with OxyContin" and featured ten big band tunes, including Count Basie's "One O'Clock Jump" and "Boogie Woogie Bugle Boy" by the Andrews Sisters.

Prior soon noticed colleagues prescribing OxyContin for chronic ailments, like back and knee pain.

Other drug companies were just as aggressively marketing pills to lower cholesterol or relieve depression. But the US Drug Enforcement Administration later said that no company had ever used this kind of branded merchandise to market a so-called Schedule II drug, an approved narcotic with a high potential for abuse and overdose.

Purdue went further, holding pain-management and speaker-training seminars in the resort communities of Boca Raton, Florida, and Scottsdale, Arizona. Some five thousand physicians, pharmacists, and nurses attended in the five years the seminars were offered. It also sponsored more than twenty thousand continuing medical education programs urging the use of timed-release opiates. Not coincidentally, OxyContin was the only such pill on the market.

In addition, Purdue funded pain organizations and websites that promoted its drug without using its name. One was Partners Against Pain, created in 1997 to offer consumers information about pain treatment options, including OxyContin. A Purdue-funded website offered doctors listings of free continuing medical educational programs on pain management.

A former Purdue sales manager for West Virginia, William Gergely, told the *South Florida Sun Sentinel* in 2003 that Purdue "told us to say things like it is 'virtually' non-addicting. That's what we were instructed to do."

It wasn't even close to true.

Looking back, it's hard to comprehend how so many smart people began to believe that this new drug was not addictive. Over the years, Americans had managed to abuse every other powerful drug. Other opiate painkillers, like Vicodin, Lorcet, and Lortab, had been sold only in small doses and combined an opioid analgesic with acetaminophen to make them hard to liquefy and inject. They caused liver damage when taken in large quantities. Yet those drugs were sold on the street for recreational use and abused.

Later, Purdue officials would say that they were surprised about OxyContin because MS Contin hadn't been abused. That wasn't entirely accurate. Certainly abuse of MS Contin never hit the levels that OxyContin would attain. But detectives in Ohio remembered that MS Contin was stolen and sold on the streets. Doctors were conned into prescribing it to drug addicts in some cities but not others—in Cincinnati but not in Columbus, for example.

Of course, MS Contin wasn't sold as a virtually risk-free panacea for chronic pain. It also didn't have a warning label like OxyContin's, which essentially gave instructions on how to abuse the pill: the label specifically told patients not to crush the tablets because that would release "a potentially toxic amount of the drug."

That was like an invitation for drug users. Addicts quickly learned to crush OxyContin and snort it or inject it, obtaining all twelve hours' worth of oxycodone at once for a euphoric high. It could also kill you. At high doses or when combined with alcohol or other drugs, Oxy-Contin slows the heartbeat and respiratory system, so much so that a person can slip into a coma and die.

One Friday shortly before Christmas in 1997, a reporter from the *Portsmouth Daily Times* decided to write a story about staying sober over the holidays. He called Ed Hughes, who ran the Counseling Center, Portsmouth's lone addiction-treatment clinic.

The reporter attended the clinic's Christmas party and interviewed some of the staff, asking especially about younger clients. Midway through, the reporter took Hughes aside.

"What's OxyContin?"

Hughes hadn't heard of it.

"Some of your clients say they're using it."

The next Monday, Hughes began asking around. His staff told him the drug had started showing up recently, that it contained a large amount of oxycodone, and that users had learned to crush it and snort it.

He called colleagues at treatment centers in northern Ohio, describing what Portsmouth was seeing. No one in Cleveland, Akron,

Columbus, or Cincinnati knew anything about OxyContin. Had Hughes made calls into the rest of Appalachia, he would have heard a far different story, one that resembled what was just getting started in Portsmouth.

But at the time, he said, "We didn't realize that we were essentially on the cutting edge of a crisis."

Around that time, Karen Charles and her husband, Jerry, were making plans to move their flooring shop into a building a few miles away in South Shore, Kentucky. Plaza Healthcare, run by Dr. Procter, was in the beige metal building next door.

In the months after relocating, they saw his business was a lot larger—and different—than they'd figured. The traffic, in fact, kept growing. Procter's waiting room could no longer accommodate the crowds. The clinic often stayed open well past its posted business hours. People parked along little Biggs Lane all day long, waiting to see him.

"They'd eat two meals in their cars," said Karen.

Many patients were from other counties, even other states, such as Missouri and Arkansas. Unsavory folks, most of them. They blocked access to the Charles Flooring parking lot. A fight once erupted between Procter clients and a truck driver blocked from making a delivery. Karen Charles never dared enter the Procter clinic, but she heard he was selling OxyContin.

By the spring of 1998, Oxy addicts were everywhere in and around Portsmouth, mostly young and white. "It was like a wildfire," Hughes remembered.

By then, Chillicothe and the surrounding towns were also awash in patients addicted to OxyContin. They would go to doctor after doctor with stories of pain and requests for more of the new drug.

The *Portsmouth Daily Times* eventually published a very different story from the one that ran after that Christmas party. The story talked about a new trend in addiction in southern Ohio and neighboring states: opiates, primarily oxycodone, delivered most prominently in that new pill called OxyContin.

PILL MILLS

By the end of the 1990s, David Procter was doing very well, at least financially.

The doctor had a $750,000 mansion, with a swimming pool, African art, and two seven-foot bronze storks. He owned a Mercedes, a Porsche, and a red Corvette—rare possessions in the Ohio River valley.

The new drug had been a rocket booster to his already booming practice. After all, OxyContin was a legitimate pharmaceutical with a legal medical use. It created addicts, and not just among those who wanted to abuse it, but among those who came in search of pain relief. Every patient who was prescribed the drug stood a chance of needing it every day.

His patients were willing to pay cash. They never missed an appointment, since they had to come to the office each month to get a doctor's prescription for Schedule II drugs. That meant a monthly-visit fee from every patient—$250 usually. And that kept waiting rooms full and cash rolling in.

Danny Colley, who grew up in Portsmouth's rough East End neighborhood, watched Procter's gradual corruption. Procter had been his family's doctor when he was a child. At twenty and fully involved in the drug world, Colley visited his former doctor's clinic. Procter by then was prescribing Xanax and Lortab for everything. Later, he became the first to prescribe OxyContin for Colley. His clinic was full.

"He was the one guy and he was burning it down," Colley said. "When he gave me my Lortabs, he said put these under your tongue and let them melt—do not snort them. When I got my first Oxys, he told me to be careful but that I could snort those. His exact words.

"I thought he was my dude! I thought he was looking out for me," Colley added. "I thought it was the coolest thing ever."

Later, he went to Procter after being injured on a job. "He got workers' comp to pay for my medicine for a year and a half," Colley said. "We all thought he was the smartest person in the world. He was brilliant, but he was a crook."

The Kentucky Board of Medical Licensure was beginning to suspect that as well. Records from the time indicated Procter was losing all control and that whatever medical ethics he once possessed had disappeared.

One upset Kentucky medical inspector, who reviewed dozens of Procter patient records during the late 1990s, used terms like "gross incompetence," "negligence," and "malpractice." Procter, the inspector wrote, didn't even record a patient's height, weight, pulse, or temperature. "Dr. Procter's records are extremely poor and I am unable to tell what exactly was prescribed in each visit from his notes," he wrote.

Of another Procter patient: "There is significant lack of evidence of evaluation and alternative treatment to this patient except for the use of controlled substances."

And another: "There did not appear to be any type of practice of medicine involved except the description of symptoms by the patient and the doctor writing for controlled substances. I do not believe this constitutes the practice of medicine."

Records showed Procter regularly prescribed Valium, Vicodin, the sedative Soma, Xanax, and a steady regimen of Redux diet pills—all with almost no diagnosis or suggestions for other treatment, such as physical therapy.

Patient complaints prompted the investigation. Three women reported they repeatedly had sex with Procter in his office, at his insistence, in exchange for prescriptions.

Then, in November 1998, Procter had a car accident. He claimed it left him with short-term memory loss, unable to practice medicine. People were skeptical. Some suggested Procter used the injuries as a ruse, saying he could no longer remember where certain patients' records were or how he had treated them.

Either way, he gave up his medical license. But he kept his pain clinic open by hiring others to do the work.

In the three years following his car accident, Procter hired fifteen doctors. They arrived with histories of drug use, previously suspended licenses, and mental problems, ready to prescribe while working for Procter for $2,500 a week. Some of these doctors learned the business and then left to set up their own pain clinics, taking with them office staff trained by Procter.

One Kentucky lawman dubbed him "Ray Kroc," for the man who spread McDonald's restaurants nationwide. Locals called him the "godfather of the pill mill." Procter's business model spread like a virus, unleashing unstable doctors on a vulnerable region.

Dr. Frederick Cohn worked for Procter before relocating to an abandoned supermarket in the town of Paintsville (pop. 3,400) in eastern Kentucky, where he saw as many as 146 patients a day, three minutes each, while lines formed outside. Cohn had preprinted prescriptions for various narcotics, including OxyContin, Lortab, Soma, and Xanax. He prescribed the same pills in the same amounts over and over throughout the day, no matter the patient's complaint—2.7 million pills in one year.

Dr. Steven Snyder worked for Procter for several months in 1999 before leaving to start his own pain clinic. Snyder, a longtime drug user, previously had his medical license suspended in Indiana and Florida for drug use. But in 1997, apparently unaware of his past, the state of Kentucky granted him an osteopath's license. While working for Procter, Snyder was addicted to Lorcet and was injecting OxyContin while writing narcotics prescriptions ten and twelve hours a day. He told a DEA investigator that he often split prescriptions with patients, supplying his habit and that of his wife.

Dr. Fortune Williams worked for Procter before moving to Garrison, Kentucky, where he worked in a clinic owned by a former Procter employee. On some days, he saw each patient for a total of ninety seconds, and he issued forty-six thousand controlled-substance prescriptions—2.3 million pills in all—in nine months.

Dr. Rodolfo Santos worked in Procter's clinic for a while, during which time at least one of his patients died. An investigator wrote that Santos displayed "gross ignorance, gross negligence, gross incompetence" and "a level of care that I would not find acceptable in a first year medical student." Santos said he knew he was dealing with addicted patients who lied and scammed drugs from him, but he was trying to educate them. "Who will help them?" he told an investigator.

Once these businesses got going, they didn't just prescribe opiate painkillers. Procter and his successors also cultivated a taste in the Rust Belt and Appalachia for the class of anti-anxiety drugs known as benzodiazepines. Valium was the first benzo, but high-dose Xanax bars were the most popular. As Procter showed his clients, benzodiazepines combined with opiates were especially potent and addictive. Both were depressants and very dangerous when taken together. But benzos seemed to enhance the euphoria of the opiates—and also make them more lethal. The combined prescription was a hot ticket at pill mills in Portsmouth and elsewhere.

Eventually, all the activity around Procter attracted the DEA in the early 2000s. The agency launched an investigation into Plaza Healthcare. Procter pleaded guilty to conspiring to distribute prescription medication in 2003; then he fled to Canada with a Cincinnati bail bondswoman who was neither his wife nor his mistress, a few days before he was to be sentenced. They were captured at the Canadian border with $40,000 and plane tickets to the Cayman Islands.

Procter was returned to Kentucky, where he had already testified against Drs. Williams and Santos in court in return for a lighter sentence in his own case. He eventually served eleven years in prison. Santos and Williams also went off to prison, as did Cohn and Snyder.

By the time the outsider doctors had been ousted and convicted, a wave of new clinics had opened, this time by local entrepreneurs. In the first years of the new century, a local junkyard owner, an attorney, a prison guard, an ex-bailiff, and a couple of convicted felons, as well as several doctors, all opened clinics, hiring doctors with permits to write the prescriptions and see patients at a rapid clip. Jody Robinson sold his car stereo shop to open a pain clinic through which he became, according to a later indictment, one of the region's biggest pill distributors.

Portsmouth became America's pill mill capital, even as OxyContin abuse was rapidly spreading across southern Ohio, West Virginia, eastern Kentucky, and beyond. Billboards for pain clinics greeted travelers along the highways entering town. For a while, Portsmouth had a pill mill for every eighteen hundred residents.

The impact of the powerful pills was hard to escape, even for the community's most prominent citizens. "My daughter was addicted," said Lisa Roberts, who became the city's public health nurse. "A judge's kid became addicted. A mayor's kid became addicted. A police chief's kid got addicted. The kids who came from excellent families got addicted." Slaves to the morphine molecule, a generation born into the town's decline set about tearing Portsmouth apart.

THE OXY TRADE

Along with pill mills that dispensed prescriptions, a new kind of business emerged: trading just about anything for pills, like a junkie's Craigslist.

Among the first of these new entrepreneurs was Mary Ann Henson, who grew up middle-class in a very religious family. She had been a cheerleader at East Portsmouth High School and the homecoming queen, but a pregnancy during her senior year derailed her.

She started using pills not long after leaving home with her newborn daughter at the end of high school. "I thought I knew everything," she said. "I was eighteen."

Henson ended up strung out and on government assistance, with food stamps and a Medicaid health-insurance card. For a while she had a boyfriend who broke into pharmacies with a group of friends. Her boyfriend went to prison, and Mary Ann was strapped for cash.

One day, a friend asked, "Hon, ain't you been to the doctor?"

The woman took her to John Lilly, who had opened the area's

second pain clinic. Lilly asked Henson to lift one knee, then the other, and the visit was over. He prescribed her a month's worth of Lorcet and Xanax. Henson gave half the pills to the woman who paid for her visit and kept half.

The woman then took her across the river to David Procter for the same charade. Henson sold her pills and a business was formed. She began going to Lilly and Procter.

When OxyContin arrived, the business grew. Henson bought the MRI images of a person with a sprained lower back. She scanned the pages into a computer and used the MRI repeatedly, changing the name on it over and over. Next, she recruited street addicts to go to the doctor, each armed with that MRI in their names. In time, Henson was driving several addicts at a time to one clinic one day, and another group of addicts to another clinic the next, waiting with them for their appointments.

Usually, each addict left with prescriptions for ninety 80 mg OxyContins—three a day, for a month. The doctor also prescribed 120 generic oxycodone 30 mg pills and 90 Xanax bars. Henson took half of the haul in exchange for driving the addict to the clinic and paying the $250 doctor's fee.

This became a classic business model in Portsmouth and elsewhere.

The biggest challenge came from turning the prescriptions into pills. Many local pharmacists wouldn't fill prescriptions from notorious clinics, so Henson and others drove the addicts to rural towns, looking for cooperative druggists.

Then there was the matter of paying between $800 and $1,200 to fill each prescription. Coming up with the cash was difficult. But if addicts qualified for state welfare payments or a federal disability program known as Supplemental Security Income (SSI), they also got a Medicaid card. With that magic card, each prescription could be filled for only a $3 co-pay, with the rest of the cost picked up by the state and federal government. A user could turn around and sell those pills for as much as $10,000 on the street.

In the county that included Portsmouth, the number of people applying for SSI each year almost doubled between 1999 and 2008, reaching a high of sixteen hundred.

The proliferation of Medicaid cards led to a proliferation of pills. And the more pills that rolled through the region, the more people grew addicted. As the business grew bigger, more people died. The Oxy black market might never have spread so quickly had addicts been forced to pay for all those pills themselves.

OxyContin had a very specific value on the street: a dollar a milligram—or, for instance, eighty dollars for one Oxy 80 mg pill. By taking half the pills from each addict, Henson could make $5,000 from each patient she took to a doctor. She sold the pills from her house with her husband, Keith. Years later they remembered their operation resembling a McDonald's drive-through. Four people on the porch waiting while ten more were doing business in the living room.

Beginning in the late 1990s and continuing for about a decade, the value of most goods in Portsmouth, and many services, was measured in pills.

Addicts ripped air conditioners out of houses for the copper wire inside. They stole manhole covers. They took large spools of copper wire from behind the school district's office. They stole their children's

Christmas presents to trade for pills. They trudged like zombies down Highway 52 in search of the next fix.

Even senior citizens saw the value of the OxyContin in their cabinets and began offering it for a profit as well. "People don't even think twice about selling," one legitimate physician remembered.

Mary Ann Henson once bought a car with OxyContin. She paid an off-duty cable TV worker in pills to install service. She paid for a dentist visit with pills. She ransomed Keith from drug-addicted kidnappers with pills. She bought steak and diapers and laundry detergent with pills. Shoes for pills. Purses for pills. Perfume for pills.

Crucially, pills also bought children's love. Junkies, whose main relationship was with dope, could briefly emerge from the fog to buy their children the toy, video game, or bracelet they coveted with pills—usually buying it off a shoplifter.

It was surprisingly easy to score almost anything. "Someone says, 'Hey, I'm looking for a chain saw,'" Henson said. "Then some guy comes by with a chain saw. You buy the chain saw for an oxycodone thirty you paid almost nothing for [thanks to your Medicaid card], and you call the other guy and sell him the chain saw for a hundred dollars cash." Soon, Henson had big-screen TVs and computers, nice furniture and power tools.

Even urine leaked into the OxyContin economy. As authorities scrutinized Scioto County doctors, some clinics began requiring occasional urine tests. Probation officers always wanted them. So a black market in clean urine emerged.

Addicts bought false bladders they strapped to their stomachs with tubes leading down into their pants. Neighbors of one pain clinic near downtown grew accustomed to people knocking on their doors, asking if they wanted to sell their urine. Outside the pill mills, people charged in pills to pee in a cup, promising clean urine as they chugged water. Kids' urine was coveted for its purity and was worth an Oxy 40 in Portsmouth for several years.

In time, a sophisticated opiate class system emerged. At the top were people who never used but sold pills and bought anything an addict brought in.

The late Jerry Lockhart was one of the elite. He lived on a promontory dubbed OxyContin Hill in West Portsmouth. He worked mostly with the so-called street rats—addicts at the bottom of the class system who could never accumulate enough cash to pay for their own doctor's visit, much less anyone else's. The town had hundreds of street rats, and more were crowding in from elsewhere on day trips to Portsmouth pill mills.

Donnie had been badly wounded in the Marines and was given morphine. He retained his taste for opiates when he returned to Portsmouth. As an Oxy addiction took hold, Donnie began selling his garage tools. He figured he sold almost all those tools to Jerry Lockhart.

During the month, he went frequently to Lockhart for pills. Lockhart would give him two, expecting four after the doctor's visit. By his doctor's visit, Donnie usually owed Lockhart almost all of what he was going to be prescribed.

Lockhart traded pills for stolen goods, which he sold out of a large garage on his property. He gave addicts pills for their food stamp cards and bought groceries with the regular payments deposited on the cards. Addicts stole goods from the store and returned the shoplifted stuff for gift cards, which they then brought to Lockhart for pills. An addict who said he worked for Lockhart claimed the dealer built virtually his entire house with material purchased with Lowe's gift cards.

Shoplifters, in fact, were the wandering peddlers in Portsmouth's junkie kingdom, providing the goods central to daily life in the Oxy-Contin economy and taking only pills in payment. They stole groceries or tampons or detergent or microwaves. And while Lowe's was an option, there was nothing quite like the Walmart in neighboring New Boston.

"You could go to Walmart and spend a half hour in there and get enough for a pill or two," said Keith Henson, Mary Ann's husband.

People put in orders and addict shoplifters delivered. On any given day, they might get orders for boys' shoes and car stereo speakers and a T-bone steak. "Walmart has such a big variety," said Angie Thuma, a former nurse who stole from Walmart for years as a street addict. "Everything was in one spot. If you need men's clothes, it was at Walmart. If you needed shoes, I stole hundreds of pairs of shoes from Walmart. It was everything a person would want in one store."

Shoplifters got pills equal to half the value of the price tag on the item. If there was no price listed on, say, a Black and Decker circular saw, Keith Henson said, "You'd call Walmart and do a price check."

Of course, the price a seller was willing to take varied by circumstances. Mary Ann once offered a junkie an oxycodone 15 for a pair of stolen Nike Air Jordan basketball shoes because the guy was too sick from withdrawal to find another buyer. She bought a refrigerator from a family with children for three 30s—$90.

But generally, if a shoplifter stole a bag of diapers, Tide detergent, DVDs, and a power sander worth about $200, he had a reasonable expectation that he would get an OxyContin 80 and an oxycodone 20.

It helped that Walmart employees displayed little love for the store and its famously low wages. Some workers were strung out themselves. Some greeters just didn't recognize what was happening. Either way, a lot of Walmart workers had no desire to face off with an addict.

"They're making ten dollars an hour," said a Portsmouth resident. "They can see the look in our faces, 'Don't get in our way.' Every now and then, you find one with a cape. One who's trying to get that manager position. The tough guy's going to try. But when I'm in withdrawal, I'm tougher."

Angie Thuma supplied a half dozen dealers with all their Christmas presents for several years running, and stole gifts for her kids as well. "For a couple months before each Christmas, I couldn't steal enough," she said. "Even if I went several times a day, I didn't have enough arms to get everything they wanted."

Christmas Day was also a big one for dealers, who opened for business awaiting addicts wanting to exchange the gifts they—or their children—received for pills.

The trade in lifted merchandise went beyond drug dealers and users. In the town's depressed, minimum-wage economy, many people needed a deal and didn't care too much where it came from. Some of Thuma's best clients were middle-aged women raising their grandkids, who couldn't get by on the money they earned.

As dealers prepared their kids to return to school in August, shoplifters fanned out, armed with long lists of school supplies and clothes and shoes in kids' sizes. One young addict wheeled flat-screen TVs through a Walmart tire shop, which had a door with no alarm. Others learned to line a purse with aluminum foil so the alarms wouldn't go off when they exited.

Other addicts would find a large box containing a child's outdoor plastic slide. They wheeled it to a secluded area of the store and emptied it. Then they would fill the now-empty box with DVD players, Xbox consoles, headphones, and Tide detergent pods. They would pay the twenty dollars that the slide cost and wheel the box to the exit. When the alarm invariably went off, they would show the greeter the receipt and be waved out.

Another veteran Walmart shoplifter told me he would wear very baggy clothing, with long john underwear underneath, taped at the ankles. He'd walk through the store, stuffing merchandise in his long johns, which would balloon out, though nothing would show under his baggy pants and shirt. "I walked out of there, it looked like I was four hundred pounds," he said.

For a long time, Walmart did not require a receipt to refund returned goods with a gift card. A $500 Walmart card was worth three OxyContin 80s—for which the dealer had paid a few dollars with a Medicaid card. A vast trade in Walmart cards kept Portsmouth's army of pill dealers in household necessities.

People in Portsmouth opened stores in their apartments that specialized in certain products, most of which they stole from Walmart: garden supplies, tools, automotive equipment. One recovering addict told me he visited the apartment of a woman who stocked everything a baby needed. "She had a bedroom you could go into set up like a store, diapers in one corner, baby food and formula, clothes on a dresser like a display table," he said. "Then she'd have boxes of high chairs and strollers."

The Oxy economy in the Ohio River valley was extreme. But by the time it was in full swing, abuse of the pills had spread way beyond the area. By 2002, US doctors—mostly primary care physicians—were prescribing more than six million OxyContin pills a year, up from just 670,000 five years before. More than a million pills were prescribed for cancer pain, compared with 250,000 in 1997. The drug now made up nearly all of Purdue Pharma's annual sales of more than $1 billion.

Meanwhile, drug rehabilitation centers filled with opiate addicts, who crowded out alcoholics seeking treatment.

"Purdue and the pharmaceutical industry were saying that addiction in OxyContin is really rare," said Dr. Carl "Rolly" Sullivan, who ran a rehab center in Morgantown, West Virginia, about 230 miles west of Portsmouth. "The incidence of addiction was far higher than they indicated."

As news reports began to describe rising OxyContin abuse and addiction, Purdue called Sullivan and asked him to speak to its sales reps. Twenty of them met with Sullivan. He spent a couple of hours with them, describing the foot traffic at his clinic and the huge amounts of their drug that addicts, some of them former pain patients, were consuming. He saw they were concerned.

"We were told this was safe," said one sales rep.

Sullivan brought along a woman from his clinic who was recovering from addiction to OxyContin. One sales rep asked her how long she would need to score OxyContin on the street outside the hotel.

"About twenty minutes," the woman replied. "But that's only because I don't drive."

Sullivan thought the visit sobered the sales reps. But Purdue kept selling OxyContin the way it always had.

Six months later, the woman that Sullivan brought to the meeting died of an OxyContin overdose.

DISCOVERY

Jaymie Mai just wanted more regular working hours when she took a job in 2000 as the chief pharmacist for the state of Washington's Department of Labor and Industries. But her job overseeing the cases of workers receiving prescription drugs for injuries took her on an unexpected path of discoveries.

Mai grew up in postwar Vietnam, the child of a South Vietnamese navy seaman imprisoned in a communist reeducation camp. In 1978, her mother took her six children aboard a small fishing boat with seventy-five other people. They floated aimlessly, besieged by Thai pirates, on a boat crammed with people retching violently, until a Malaysian merchant ship happened by and took them aboard.

A year later, Mai and her family were on a plane to Seattle and a new life. She earned a pharmacy degree at the University of Washington and worked at several hospitals. Somewhere in there, she developed an intense need for neatness and order. She cleaned her house a lot because it helped her reduce stress and think things through. She loved to garden and planted roses outside the new house that she and her husband bought when she got the new job.

She came to Labor and Industries without a strong opinion on the growing use of opiates in medicine. In the hospitals where she worked, opiates were used for broken legs or following surgery, which she believed appropriate.

Her department generated enormous amounts of data about worker injuries and deaths. The state of Washington provides workers' compensation insurance for two-thirds of the state's 1.2 million workers, handling claims when workers are injured or disabled on the job. The state also oversees the rest, those workers at companies big enough to provide the insurance in-house.

As narcotic painkillers became more widely used for chronic pain, doctors prescribed more and more of the drugs to workers. One part of Mai's job involved making sure that doctors were documenting whether the new opiate painkillers were helping to reduce patients' pain and improve their ability to function. Otherwise, why should the state keep paying for the drugs?

There, more than twenty-five hundred miles away from the pill mills in Portsmouth, she saw for the first time how the drugs were used for chronic pain. What she saw was alarming: "It was automatic: 'You hurt? Let me write you a prescription for opioids,'" she said. "They were treating patients with opioids and the patient would come in with more complaints of pain a month later and they would up the dose."

The next appointment would be scheduled, but no one seemed to be asking questions, she said. "I could see in the medical record that the provider wasn't checking to see if the drug was even helping them. The patient would come in every visit complaining of more pain.

"Nobody ever said, 'Wait a minute. Time out. Let's figure out what's going on.'"

The cases crossing her desk grew. "Fifty, a hundred cases a month," she said. "But there's no attempt to document if the drug was working, one, or, two, if they even are appropriate candidates to receive opioids. Did they try a nonopioid first?"

Six months into the job, Mai noticed something even more shocking: workers were dying from these very painkillers. This wasn't supposed to happen. Yet one case after another appeared in her data—all overdoses. In a typical year, fifty or more workers in the state died, mostly from accidents—electrocutions or falls, for instance—or from job-related cancers. Now, workers with a sprained back or knee were dying.

She asked Gary Franklin, the department's medical director, what they should be doing.

Franklin had been an opiate skeptic from the start. He had a master's degree in public health and had taught several years as a professor of neurology and preventive medicine at the University of Colorado. He had joined the department in 1988 and heard the arguments that the drugs were less addictive than was thought. He was there when a state medical commission removed legal sanctions against doctors for prescribing narcotics in the course of acceptable medical practice.

Now, two years after the change, Mai was seeing opiate-overdose deaths. Franklin still had questions. Were these workers dying from recreational abuse of opiates or from pills they'd been prescribed?

More information was needed: death certificates, coroner autopsy reports, drug prescriptions for each person who died. Over the next two years, in a back room in the department's second floor, Mai pored over cases of workers dying from opiate overdoses. At home, she relentlessly tended her growing and increasingly ornate rose garden.

Tracking down the cases was the first task. Some 266 people in the workers' comp system had died since 1995. She whittled this down to sixty where drugs were mentioned, and ordered the doctors' records, death certificates, and the autopsy reports for each.

She and Franklin found that forty-four people with chronic pain in Washington's workers' comp system had died definitely, probably, or possibly from prescription opiate use between 1995 and 2002. Most had died after 1999, the year the state's intractable pain regulation was written. Most were men; most were under fifty years old. They had come to workers' comp with non-life-threatening ailments—back pain or carpal tunnel syndrome, say—for which they were prescribed opiates, and they were dead a short while later.

Mai and Franklin also found that prescriptions for the strongest opiates more than doubled. The number of prescriptions for much milder pain relievers dropped or remained the same. Faced with patient pain, doctors were going right to the heavy artillery, and that meant, beginning in about 1997, OxyContin.

It was a stunning discovery.

In August 2001, about the time Jaymie Mai was discovering painkiller overdoses, John Brownlee took the job of US attorney for the western district of Virginia.

The office was a small one, with only twenty-four attorneys. But it was located near the gathering opiate storm circling over Appalachia.

Brownlee had a sterling Republican Party pedigree. His father had once been secretary of the army. He was being mentioned as a possible future governor of Virginia or a state attorney general.

As US attorney, he began to realize that people were dying of overdoses across the states of Kentucky, West Virginia, Ohio, and southern Virginia. Other prosecutors' offices were indicting notorious pill mill doctors, David Procter among them. Brownlee's office prosecuted a Roanoke doctor named Cecil Knox, who state records showed was a prolific prescriber of OxyContin.

From there, Brownlee said, "We looked at this and said we should take a look at the company marketing this stuff."

He subpoenaed all Purdue's records related to marketing OxyContin. There were millions of pages and e-mails. Federal employees took up residence in a conference room on a floor of Purdue headquarters in Stamford, Connecticut, and copied company files for months.

Brownlee said the records showed that the company was training salespeople to sell OxyContin as if it were nonaddictive and did not provoke withdrawal symptoms. Physicians, therefore, could feel comfortable prescribing it for many kinds of pain.

"One of the pieces of evidence that was looked at were 'call notes,'" he said. "The company had a process in which salesmen would go to a doctor, then summarize what was discussed. That went back to a central clearinghouse."

Those records of sales calls showed a pattern: "They were trained to sell the drug in a way that was simply not accurate," he said. It wasn't just a few salesmen or in certain regions, he said. "It was an extremely high percentage of sales reps in various states who were making these allegations. This was done in all fifty states. That's when you rise to corporate culpability."

But building a legal case and getting all the facts in line is a slow, methodical process. Brownlee's team wouldn't be ready to file its lawsuit until 2006.

For Mai and Franklin, turning their data into a paper in an established medical journal also was a long process. Their conclusions would be the first documentation in the United States showing that people were dying because of the practice of prescribing opiates for noncancer pain. But it wouldn't be published until 2005.

By then, the cycle of abuse and addiction had entered a new phase. OxyContin abusers were moving in large numbers to a new, cheaper drug, one even more powerful and addictive than pills: heroin.

PART 2
Heroin

ENRIQUE

The first home Enrique remembered was a cardboard-and-plywood shack with a corrugated-tin roof at the bottom of a rancho, an outpost away from cities and towns. Though the rancho was near the city of Tepic, in the small western state of Nayarit in Mexico, there were no paved streets and no electricity. His parents eked out a living selling charcoal and wood.

Enrique was their second child of four. Enrique's early memories are sparse: yelling, his father beating his mother, and his mother having no idea where each day's food was coming from.

Then, a miracle. Enrique's father inherited all fifty acres owned by his parents. Now a landowner, he grew sugarcane. With better circumstances, his father added arrogance to his anger. Coming home drunk at night, he yelled at his kids and beat his wife more often. His truck roared like a beast, and he rode around the village high in the seat, as if it were a fine mare.

One morning, when Enrique was eight, he was helping his father, who was hungover and working under the truck. His father called for his son to find a tool. As Enrique searched desperately, his father grew angry and crawled out from under the truck. Enrique tried to run off, but his father chased him down and beat him. Enrique cried himself to sleep that night, angry that his mother hadn't defended him, hating life and his father.

Growing up in an area known as the Toad, Enrique never knew anybody poor who wasn't miserable. At school, teachers treated kids from the village's upper barrio with respect but spoke sharply to the ragged children who came from the Toad without food for lunch. Some teachers forbade the Toad kids from going to the bathroom until they wet themselves. A few teachers showed up drunk; others didn't show up for weeks at a time. Enrique's father mocked him for not knowing his multiplication tables, but how could he know them with teachers like these?

Life held one thrill: his mother's brothers were up in Los Angeles working, which gave his family a connection that other kids envied. Villagers spoke of his uncles like far-off explorers. But Enrique's father never got along with these uncles. As in many ranchos, extended families lived nearby and intense family feuds were common. Years before, there had been a fight. His father, on one side, was knifed. On the other side, two people from his uncles' family died.

Over time, his mother saved enough to buy a cow, and finally they were ranchers of a sort. His father reminded him that he, the only boy, would someday inherit the land and the house. Soon enough, though, it began to feel more like a threat, tethering him to a lifetime of poverty. He became determined to escape that fate.

His urgency intensified when he fell for a girl. She was twelve and beautiful. Her father was a butcher, in the upper classes of the rancho, well above Enrique's station as the son of an alcoholic sugarcane farmer. Enrique knew he could not give this girl the life she, and her father, expected for herself. But when he asked her to be his girlfriend, she accepted. Theirs was an innocent village romance, filled with kisses and hugs. For it to become more than that, Enrique knew he would have to get moving.

His mother found work overseeing the village school's lunch program, so Enrique no longer went hungry at school. His father was elected treasurer of the local sugarcane farmers' cooperative. He oversaw the installation of the first village streetlights. Enrique was surprised to see his father so diligent about putting in village light poles while he brought so much darkness home.

Then junior high ended. Enrique attempted high school in Tepic, a city of 330,000 only a few miles away but seemingly in another country. He spent two weeks there, each day without anything to eat for lunch, before he ran out of bus money and withdrew.

The threat of a life in the fields now seemed frighteningly real. He would never be able to give his girl what she and her father expected for her. In the village, girls married young; though she was only thirteen, Enrique had no time to lose. He secretly made plans to join his uncles in Canoga Park, California.

One day he walked through the village, greeted his friends, and spent time with his girlfriend. The next, he took his birth certificate and put on his best black jacket, a white collared shirt, and blue pants; he kissed his mother and said he'd be back later that day. He went to Tepic and boarded Tres Estrellas de Oro, the low-cost bus line that over the years took north hundreds of thousands of Mexicans intending to cross the border.

He paid for the ticket with two hundred pesos he had swiped from his parents. He considered the money a loan so he wouldn't feel bad for taking it. He sat by the window for twenty-eight hours so he could see all the things he had never seen before.

It was 1989 and he was fourteen.

The chaotic border city of Tijuana, Mexico, was the biggest place Enrique had ever seen. Thousands of people flowed like a river through the central bus station before crossing into the United States.

Enrique slept in the bus terminal and wandered the streets during the day. He found a coyote, a smuggler who took people into the US, and asked the price to Canoga Park. When he told the man he had no address but figured he'd just ask around, the coyote laughed.

"Canoga Park is huge. It's not like your rancho."

Still, he hung on for several days. Finally, famished, his prized clothes filthy and stinking, and his money almost gone, he dialed the village's telephone in tears. On a second call, his hysterical mother answered. His uncles would come for him.

They arranged for him to cross the border posing as the son of a man with papers. Two mornings later, Enrique was in an uncle's apartment in the San Fernando Valley.

"Now," the uncle said, "I'll give you a thousand dollars and a suitcase and you'll go home."

"No, what I want from life you can't buy with a thousand dollars."

His uncles took him to eat and then to another apartment. One uncle opened a closet and there, like a glorious revelation, were dozens of pairs of Levi's 501s, with labels and price tags attached.

"Take what you want."

With that, the boy who had never had more than two threadbare pairs of pants now had his first new, tough dark-blue 501s. Much later he would remember the first time he bought a pair for himself in America, and then the first time he came home wearing 501s.

Back home, Enrique had always assumed his uncles were working hard in some honorable trade. Now they sat him down. One uncle pulled out a shoebox filled with golf-ball-sized chunks of a dark, sticky substance and balloons of every color.

"What's that?" Enrique asked.

"*Chiva*," his uncle said. "Goat," the Mexican slang term for black tar heroin. "This is how we make our money."

In the mountains to the south of Tepic and Enrique's rancho in Xalisco County, Cora Indian *campesinos*—small farmers—grew poppies. They harvested the opium goo from the flowers and sold it to cookers. A newly cooked kilo of vinegary, sticky chiva would head north in a boom box or a backpack within a couple of days, virtually uncut, and would often hit LA streets only a week after the goo was drawn from the poppy.

The process dated back to 1874, when Dr. Alder Wright first synthesized diacetylmorphine in London in an attempt to find a nonaddictive form of morphine to relieve pain. In 1898, a Bayer Laboratory chemist in Germany, Heinrich Dreser, reproduced Wright's diacetylmorphine and called it heroin—for *heroisch*, German for "heroic," the word that Bayer workers used to describe how it made them feel when Dreser tested it on them.

Heroin was first believed to be nonaddictive. Heroin pills were marketed as a remedy for coughs and respiratory ailments. As addicts ever since have discovered, heroin is constipating and was thus marketed as an antidiarrheal. Women used it, on doctor's orders, for menstrual cramps. With few other drugs at hand, doctors prescribed it for pain or disease. Addiction exploded—to a drug that doctors had said was safe.

The high rate of addition led to the Harrison Narcotics Tax Act of 1914. The law taxed and regulated opiates while allowing doctors to use them in medicine. But it was transformed when police started arresting doctors for prescribing opiates to addicts.

Physicians soon stopped prescribing the drugs, and addicts turned to crime.

A government campaign demonizing "dope fiends" followed, aided by a compliant media. The addict was a deviant, a crime-prone, weak-willed moral failure. This idea informed the view of junkies for decades. The mythic figure of the heroin pusher also emerged. He supposedly lurked around schoolyards and candy stores, giving young people habit-forming dope, hoping for future customers.

Heroin—originally imported from Turkey, Afghanistan, or Southeast Asia—replaced morphine on the streets. It was simple to make and cheaper than morphine. It was also more concentrated and thus easier to hide and more profitable to dilute by cutting it with other substances. An addict craved heroin several times a day, so he was a terrific customer.

In the 1930s, users began injecting weak heroin, diluted with other substances. Injecting maximized the euphoria but also led to nasty public health problems—among them, later, ferocious rates of hepatitis C and HIV.

Mexican black tar was more concentrated and was usually sold undiluted. Because tar is a semiprocessed, less-filtered form of heroin, it added to the health issues. The impurities in the drug clog addicts' veins when injected. Unable to find working veins, addicts shoot it into their muscles. "Muscling" black tar heroin, in turn, leads to infections, rotting skin, botulism, even gangrene.

In the apartment in Canoga Park, Enrique's uncle rolled little pieces of the sticky gunk into balls the size of BBs. He put each one in a tiny balloon and tied the balloon shut. Finally, he wrapped the telephone in a towel to mute the ring. When he plugged in the phone, the calls started coming.

These are customers, his uncle explained. Guys are out there driving around all day with these balloons. We give each caller a different intersection to meet a driver. Then we beep a driver the code for the intersection where that customer will be. We do this all day long.

"We wouldn't have told you had you not showed up," his uncle said.

Enrique begged to work for them. You're too young, said one uncle. But Enrique pleaded and finally the uncles relented.

The San Fernando Valley comprises 260 square miles, larger than Chicago, and contains the sprawling northern chunk of Los Angeles. Canoga Park, with sixty thousand people, is on the west end. Once a mostly white area with modest suburban ranch-style houses, it was rapidly becoming mostly Mexican.

Enrique was tall enough not to arouse suspicion behind the wheel. He drove the streets of the San Fernando Valley with his mouth full of tiny balloons, following instructions from his uncles. Those first weeks he remembered like a fairy tale, as if everything he had heard about America was true: money, clothes, and good food seemed as plentiful as the sunshine.

At the apartment, he turned on a VCR and a porno film leaped to life. His uncles ate often at a seafood restaurant. They drank at a local bar that Nayarit immigrants frequented; as long as Enrique was with them, the waitresses served him beer.

After a few months, the uncles installed him in an apartment on De Soto Avenue and gave him the keys to two cars. He would run the business—roll the heroin into balloons, take calls, direct drivers on the street. The phone rang all day until he shut it down at eight p.m. As he turned fifteen, he was taking orders for $5,000 worth of heroin a day. He collected stolen 501s and VCRs and porno films that addicts exchanged for dope.

Enrique no longer had to worry about his jeans fading when he washed them. There were always more. He showered with fragrant shampoo, and exchanged the village pond for the swimming pool at an uncle's house in a neighborhood full of Americans. His clients were nurses and lawyers—one of his best clients was a wealthy lawyer—prostitutes, former soldiers who'd been to Vietnam, old junkies from the barrio, and young cholos, or gang members.

Back home, drug users were the moral equivalents of pedophiles. But drug sales were his pathway out of *problemas*, the shootings and family fights that regularly boiled over in the rancho. The 501s didn't hurt either.

For seven months he worked for his uncles in Canoga Park. Finally, they packed him a suitcase, gave him $2,000, and sent him home.

Dozens of villagers welcomed Enrique home to his isolated rancho and the Toad, a few miles outside the town of Xalisco, Nayarit. He was admired for crossing the border alone. He gave his money to his mother, keeping two hundred dollars.

Older folks besieged him with questions. A few friends asked for help finding the kind of work he was doing. He put them off but saw that apparently word had spread more than his uncles had realized. He wanted to get back to California himself in a few months.

He was only fifteen and people were coming to him for favors. It was a luxurious feeling.

TIENDITAS

The morning after Enrique's big homecoming party, his mother was happy and his father held his tongue. California gave Enrique a new option. If his father mistreated him, he'd leave again. So they ate together as a family and tried to forget past misery now that their new Northerner, as they called him, had come home.

Still, Enrique could think of nothing but California. He wanted a rematch.

Other kids were now going north the way he had. The retail system that Xalisco immigrants like Enrique's uncles were devising in the San Fernando Valley allowed even the humblest to do more than just dream. Everyone could have his own business, be his own boss. By risking a lot, young men added to their status back home.

Around 1991, Enrique got another chance. An uncle called from the San Fernando Valley and offered him work with good pay. This time Enrique arrived confident and brash, proud of his worldliness, no longer the scared village kid.

He saw immediately why his uncles had called. More heroin dealers from the *municipio*, Xalisco County, were crowding into the San Fernando Valley market. Though the county had just forty-nine thousand residents, hundreds of young people from the necklace of communities and ranchos near the town of Xalisco were coming north. Competition was intensifying. Prices were dropping.

Of course, David Tejeda and his brothers were there. Tejeda was among the first from Xalisco County to sell heroin in Southern California and was among the first to display what black tar heroin could do for a ranchero kid. His horses were the finest in the county, and he was a master at making them hop and prance to a banda's staccato beat.

Beto Sánchez and the Sánchez clan were growing big. So, too, were Beto Bonque and his family, as well as the Bernals. The Langaricas—brothers Julio, Chuy, and Tino, whose father was a witch doctor back in Xalisco—had cells, as did their cousins, the Garcia-Langaricas, Polla and Macho. One family had Pasadena to itself.

Each family had two or three cells going, and each cell had at least a couple of drivers working shifts from six a.m. to noon and noon to six p.m. every day. At night, drivers met at apartments to roll heroin into balloons for the next day.

It was not a glamorous business. You were there to work, said the family bosses, who paid each driver $600 a week and wanted every hour accounted for. The cell owners changed the drivers in and out, moving them into apartments and out again six months later, switching cars even more frequently, and ordering drivers to hand out beeper numbers to junkies on the street along with free samples.

His uncles promised Enrique more money and a new truck in Mexico if he did well. With another driver, Enrique patrolled the streets of the San Fernando Valley, looking for addicts. He'd give them a free sample and a phone number. Within a few weeks, he raised the daily take to $5,000.

Then, early one morning, police raided an uncle's house. In the weeks that followed, Enrique saw his remaining uncles falter. Gang members robbed their drivers and they did nothing. Several times clients put knives to Enrique's throat. He spit the balloons into their hands, remembering a saying from his father: "Die for what's yours, but not for what's others'."

More people arrived from Xalisco, and the number of heroin *tienditas*—small stores—multiplied. Workers left bosses to start their own cells. A friend Enrique knew from Xalisco came up and started his own network.

Then El Gato, an especially aggressive dealer, surprised everyone. He took an addict and chiva and opened a heroin cell down in San Diego. Before long, Enrique heard, El Gato had one going up in Portland as well. The Tejedas had a store going in Hawaii. Suddenly, the Nayarit group realized they could find new markets far from the Valley.

Enrique, now sixteen, took it all in. As his uncles' network floundered, he and a friend bought a car and rented an apartment on the sly. For a while, without his uncles' knowledge, he ran his own heroin tiendita on the side. But then a gang member robbed him, took his dope, and cut him. His uncles discovered his side business. They beat him, gave him $1,800 as payment for his months of work, and sent him back to Nayarit.

With that, the one escape from a life of sugarcane farming seemed closed to him forever. His sisters smiled at the gifts he brought, but he felt their disappointment. He went to work again in the fields with his father, who smirked and mocked him.

As if to show up his son, his father installed a satellite dish outside the family shack, one way a family announced that it had arrived. His family had no decent bathroom, Enrique wryly observed, but it had a satellite dish. Still, his father was happy.

Without the heroin trade, Enrique couldn't imagine a life where he controlled his own decisions. Harvest time came and Enrique made fifty pesos a load trucking the towering stacks of cut sugarcane to the mill. The heat sapped him, and he arrived home every night looking like he had been tossed in a bag of charcoal, thinking to himself, "I'm leaving my soul in these fields."

Just as he despaired of ever finding a way out, a cell boss called and offered Enrique a job as a driver in Phoenix.

He kissed his mother and took a bus to Arizona.

This was his chance. Within a week, he knew the Phoenix streets, and before long he was running the store himself—cutting up the heroin, answering the beeper, and driving to deliver the balloons to the clients. His customers were mostly women: lawyers, nurses, a prostitute or two. He soon raised the store's daily take from $1,200 to $3,000. He worked from eight a.m. to nine p.m., grabbed a hamburger at a drive-through, and was at home by ten p.m. to balloon up the heroin for the next day. He didn't have time to wash his clothes. But he made $5,000 that month.

One day, his suppliers in Phoenix told him the boss would be arriving that night from Xalisco. As Enrique headed home, his beeper buzzed. The big boss wanted McDonald's—a fish sandwich—before the meeting. Enrique scurried to get the food. He walked into the apartment to discover that two gunmen had his boss and his suppliers in their underwear and on their knees in the bathroom.

The invaders had found two ounces of heroin, jewelry, and some cash. Yet when they demanded more, and placed a gun to his head, Enrique kept silent.

That morning, he had packed tens of thousands of dollars in stacks of cash but had no time to do anything with it. He put it at the bottom of a trash bag overflowing with the detritus of his fast-food diet—old french fries, pizza crusts, used paper plates, and soda cans. If he told the gunmen about the money, it would look like he'd set it all up. So he took their pistol-whipping in silence, and they left with only $5,000 and those ounces of heroin. They left behind $80,000 at the bottom of that garbage bag.

The boss, grateful for Enrique's loyalty, pulled him off the street and gave him two heroin drivers to supervise. Enrique worked harder. Business boomed. He sent money to his family to begin building a house for himself. When telephone service finally came to the Toad, he paid to make sure his family had a line installed in their house. Three months after the robbery, Enrique was ready to return home.

He bought a $1,000 pair of boots and a $500 hat at a Phoenix western wear store and boarded a bus home with $15,000 in his pocket. In the luggage compartment, he had stowed duffel bags bulging with clothes, jewelry, shoes, and VCRs. For so long he had sought this magnificent return.

The clothes he brought home were Levi's 501s, Guess, Tommy Hilfiger, and Polo—measures of his success. At fifteen, Enrique had helped his family survive; now, at eighteen, the heroin he sold in Phoenix allowed him to provide for them entirely.

His family gathered him up at the bus station in Tepic. In their rancho, across the road from his childhood home, his new house was under construction, paid for with the money he had sent. It had two bedrooms, a full kitchen, a garage with an automatic door, a roof that didn't leak, and an indoor bathroom. He felt at that moment that everything was possible, and he wanted to cry.

Later, in his room with his mother, he pulled the cash out of his pocket and more from his sock. It fluttered onto the bed.

"Did you rob someone?"

"No," he said, smiling broadly. "It's mine."

She didn't ask how he got it. He was sure she imagined. That night, he would always remember, was the first time his family had more than enough to eat. He brought out shirts, dresses, toys. His youngest sister called him Dad.

For the next two years, he split his time between his village and Phoenix, running his boss's heroin crews on the streets. He bought a used black Mercury Cougar. He took his girlfriend and his family to Tepic's best restaurants. He put his sister through college—the first graduate in their family. His mother no longer asked her husband for money to feed the family, nor endured his blows and insults in exchange.

That year at the Feria del Elote (Corn Festival) in August, Enrique and a friend who worked with him in Arizona owned the central plaza in Xalisco. Usually rancheros would save all year to pay for only one hour of banda music in the plaza, but Enrique and his friend paid a banda $3,000 to play all night. They drank and offered alcohol to anyone who showed up. They only stopped because Mass at the cathedral was about to begin on Sunday morning.

It did not, however, endear Enrique to his girlfriend's father, who was happy to sell meat to his mother but didn't want an uneducated kid from the Toad, a chiva dealer, for a son-in-law. The butcher had been friendly when Enrique was a boy, but he hadn't spoken to him since Enrique took up with his daughter.

As the years passed, Enrique returned occasionally to Phoenix, then did a stint in Portland, then went back home again. He began to feel unsettled. His salary wasn't bad, but his expenses had risen. His ambitions were greater. He had a car but wanted a new one. He'd taken orders all his life and wanted to know how it felt to be the boss.

He was twenty-two and ready to marry. His girlfriend's parents would never allow it. She was still in high school.

So, one day in 1996, he took 10,000 pesos, $1,000, and his Beretta 9mm and filled the Cougar with gas. He went to his girlfriend's school and drove her off to Puerto Vallarta, stealing her from her parents. It was the village way of marrying against the parents' wishes.

When she realized what was happening, she put up a fight at first, insisting on lots of conditions, all of which he agreed to. He took her to the Hotel Krystal, which he remembered later for the first valet service he'd ever used. When they returned, in the eyes of the rancho, they were as good as married, no matter what her parents said.

He took her to his new house to live. Then he set off to Albuquerque, New Mexico, where he had heard black tar heroin would find a market, and he a future.

DELIVERED LIKE PIZZA

As a street cop, Dennis Chavez had long heard about a place called Nayarit in Mexico that was supplying local Mexican American drug dealers with heroin.

For a long time, though, the place didn't mean much to Chavez, a former college football player who stood six feet four and favored Harleys. Then he joined the Denver Police Department's narcotics unit in 1995 and started hearing about Nayarit all the time.

The men from Nayarit sold a substance that was different from the light-brown, highly diluted powder that had long dominated the local heroin trade. This heroin was dark and sticky and looked like Tootsie Rolls or rat feces. They called it black tar.

By the mid-1990s, black tar had replaced the old powder in Denver, and Mexican dealers had replaced Mexican Americans. Mexicans were arrested at the bus station with backpacks and a kilo or two of the drug. But Chavez still had no sense of how this fit together, if it did at all.

Then one day, an informant said to him, "You know they're all from the same town, right?"

The informant said that what Chavez had been seeing on the streets—dealers, couriers with backpacks of heroin, drivers with balloons of heroin—all looked very random and scattered, but it was not. It was all connected.

They're all from a town called Xalisco—Ha-LEES-koh—the informant told him. Not to be confused with a state in Mexico pronounced the same way but spelled with a *J*. The informant had never been there but believed Xalisco to be a small place, a town with a few small villages near it.

These guys running around have a simple system for selling heroin retail, he said, which relied on cheap, illegal Mexican labor, just the way a fast-food joint did. From then on, Chavez pumped the informant, at bars and in a truck outside the man's house, about this system, which seemed to be unique in the drug underworld.

Think of it like a fast-food franchise, the informant said, or a pizza delivery service. Each heroin cell or franchise has an owner in Xalisco, Nayarit, who supplies the cell with heroin. The owner doesn't often come to the United States. He communicates only with the cell manager, who lives in Denver and runs the business.

Beneath the cell manager is a telephone operator, who takes phone orders from addicts. Under the operator are several drivers, paid a weekly wage and given housing and food. With their mouths full of twenty-five or thirty tiny balloons of heroin at a time, they look like chipmunks.

If police pull them over, they swig water and swallow the balloons. The balloons remain intact in the body and are eliminated in the driver's poop. They also keep more balloons hidden in the car.

The operator's phone number is circulated among heroin addicts. Once an order is taken, the operator tells customers where to meet the driver: some suburban shopping center parking lot—a McDonald's, a Wendy's, a CVS pharmacy. (Before cell phones were common, the operators used codes and pagers to relay messages to the drivers.)

A driver swings by the parking lot and the addict pulls out to follow him, usually down side streets. The driver stops and the addict jumps into the driver's car. There, in broken English and broken Spanish, a cross-cultural heroin deal is cut, with the driver spitting out the balloons the addict wants and taking his cash.

Drivers do this all day, the guy said, usually eight a.m. to eight p.m. A new cell of drivers can quickly gross $5,000 a day, which can grow to $15,000 a day within a year.

The cells compete with each other, but they're never violent, the informant said. They never carry guns. They work hard at blending in. They don't party where they live. They drive sedans that are several years old and switch them out regularly.

None of the workers use the drug. Drivers spend a few months in a city and then the bosses send them home or to a cell in another town. New drivers are coming up all the time, usually farm boys from Xalisco County. The informant assumed there were thousands of these kids back in Nayarit, aching to come north and drive some US city with their mouths packed with heroin balloons.

To a degree unlike any other narcotics operation, he said, Xalisco cells run like legitimate businesses. The cell owner pays each driver a salary—$1,200 a week was the going rate in Denver at the time. Their cars, their apartments, their phones were all company owned. A fixed paycheck meant the drivers didn't have any incentive to dilute the heroin to improve profits, as previous dealers did.

To build the business, drivers are also encouraged to offer special deals: $15 per balloon or seven for $100. A free balloon on Sunday to an addict who buys Monday through Saturday. Selling heroin a tenth of a gram at a time is their one and only, full-time, seven-days-a-week job, and that includes Christmas Day, since heroin addicts need their dope every day.

But ask to buy a large quantity of dope, the informant said, and you'll never hear from them again. That really startled the informant. He knew of no other Mexican trafficking group that preferred to sell tiny quantities.

Moreover, because of prejudices groomed in the ranchos, the Xalisco cells never deal with African Americans. They don't sell or buy from blacks, who they fear will rob them.

What the informant described, Chavez could see, amounted to a major innovation in the US drug underworld. Guys from Xalisco had figured out that what white people—especially middle-class white kids—wanted most was service and convenience. They didn't want to go to some seedy dope house or neighborhood to buy their drugs. So the guys from Xalisco would deliver it to them.

By the mid-1990s, Chavez's informant counted a dozen major metro areas in the western United States where cells from tiny Xalisco, Nayarit, operated. In Denver, he could count eight or ten cells, each with three or four drivers, working daily. They were spreading like a virus, quietly and unrecognized by many in law enforcement, who often mistook Xalisco franchises for isolated groups of small-time dealers.

"I call them the Xalisco Boys," Chavez said. "They're nationwide."

Like so many Mexican immigrants, the men from Xalisco weren't in the United States to build a new life. Instead, they imagined going home for good.

This was the American Dream for many Mexican immigrants: to return to Mexico better off than they had left it. They called home and sent money constantly. They were usually far more involved in, say, the digging of a new well in the rancho than in the workings of the school their children attended in the United States. They returned home for the village's annual fiesta and spent money they couldn't afford on barbecues, weddings, and quinceañeras.

Even as they worked the toughest jobs in America, they built houses in the rancho back home. These houses might take a decade to finish and often had wrought-iron gates, modern plumbing, and marble floors. Immigrants added to them each time they returned.

But the Xalisco Boys were different. Their work generated more cash, which they lavished on family. Their homes went up in a few months instead of over years. By the mid-1990s, they had set off a construction boom in Xalisco County.

And, said the former wife of a cell boss, there was something else: after building their houses and providing for their families, what the guys seemed to want most of all were Levi's 501s.

Levi's 501s were the ultimate clothing status symbol for men in Mexico's ranchos in the 1990s. They were very expensive in Mexico. But thanks to addicts willing to shoplift, drivers could get them cheaply in the US. Addicts were willing to take orders according to size and color and trade them, two pairs of 501s for twenty dollars' worth of black tar.

While she was married into the Xalisco world, "it was more about the jeans than anything," she said. "They had stacks of jeans. They'd bring back home exactly the sizes people wanted."

The brand-new Levi's 501s, in turn, inspired many youngsters—who had only thin, cheap jeans, if they had any at all—to hire on as drivers.

Every trafficker's return was like Christmas Day, as relatives lined up for gifts, especially those jeans. Some traffickers came pulling trailers full of clothes. "The family wants more and more and more, so the guys start feeling the pressure," the former wife said. "My ex used to send all kinds of clothes home. First it was 501s, but then later it was 'I want Guess jeans,' then Tommy Hilfigers."

The Feria del Elote in August was another highlight. "That's when you get to show off the most," she said. "It's like a kid going to Disneyland for the first time. They walk around with their chest out. Everybody looks at them."

Thus with an addict's energy and single-mindedness, she said, the Xalisco Boys sought new markets with higher profit margins, awaiting the chance to go back home, to be the kings of their dreamland for a week or two.

In Boise, Idaho, Ed Ruplinger was coming to the same realization as Dennis Chavez in Denver: the Xalisco Boys had taken over the heroin trade.

Ruplinger, a Boise narcotics investigator, noticed his drug task force was suddenly arresting lots of young Mexicans. But the men never did much jail time, since they had only a small quantity of drugs and no weapons. More frustrating, no matter how many Nayarit heroin drivers his task force arrested, more drivers filled the open slots.

In fact, arrests seemed to only increase the competition. For a while, the local drug dealer seemed to be Cesar Garcia-Langarica, a trim Mexican in his mid-forties who was known as Polla. Then, just before Christmas 1996, a sharp-eyed postal inspector came upon a package that alerted a drug-sniffing dog. Inside was a Santa Claus doll. Inside the doll was black tar heroin.

The narcotics task force scheduled the parcel's delivery. Soon after, a Boise drug team burst in and found four well-dressed, middle-aged Mexican men sitting around a card table already breaking up the heroin into small packets. They, too, were all from the state of Nayarit—last name of Tejeda.

In the aftermath of the Santa Claus bust, crew after crew descended on the town to compete with Polla. "Polla was one of the founding fathers. He comes in and sets it all up," Ruplinger said later. "The word gets out back home. Then every operative in Nayarit ends up moving in."

He struggled to keep up with the growing trade, finally getting permission to wiretap Polla's phone. Keen to keep competitors at bay, Polla insisted that his drivers provide excellent customer service. Once when a driver reported a customer complaint of a bad batch of dope, Polla promised to make it right; the driver delivered better-quality stuff to the client the next day.

Ruplinger also discovered Boise was part of a much bigger drug ring. Polla had left Denver, complaining he couldn't make money there because of the competition. But he had crews in Portland, Oregon; Salt Lake City, Utah; and Honolulu, Hawaii. If Boise had a half dozen cells, he wondered, how many crews must Denver have? What about Portland?

In Portland, in fact, there were nine cells operating by the late 1990s, each with three drivers rotating in and out.

Paul "Rock" Stone, an FBI agent, did some math. Each tenth of a gram in Portland sold for about fifteen dollars. The cells were grossing about $150,000 a kilo. Informants told him that it cost about $2,000 to produce a kilo of black tar heroin in Nayarit. In Portland, their overhead was cheap apartments, old cars, gas, food, and $500 a week for each driver.

Profit per kilo, Stone figured, was well over $100,000.

The cost to Portland was far greater. Addiction rates were climbing. A local detox center was accustomed to seeing forty-year-old heroin addicts, with just 5 to 10 percent of patients hooked on the powerful drug. Then, around 1994 to 1995, the center began to see twenty-three-year-old heroin addicts. Within a couple of years, more than 50 percent of its clients were addicted to the street drug.

Moreover, fatal overdoses had surged. That wasn't obvious until Gary Oxman, the chief health officer for Multnomah County, dug into the data and discovered that autopsy physicians were each describing heroin overdoses differently.

The inconsistent language had masked a frightening trend. In 1991, the county had ten heroin overdose deaths. But starting in 1996, more than one hundred people a year were dying from heroin.

"By the time we discovered it," Oxman said years later, "it wasn't a new wave at all."

Not long after, Oxman said, competition among the Xalisco cells brought prices down so far, "you could maintain a moderate heroin habit for about the same price as a six-pack of premium beer" per day.

THE MAN

The men from Nayarit pioneered the first wave of the Xalisco method of selling heroin. The Man, an American who adopted Nayarit as his own, ignited the second.

The Man grew up in California, spending his teen years in a barrio in the San Fernando Valley. He dropped out of Van Nuys High and soon was dealing marijuana, cutting up pounds of weed and selling joints in the neighborhood. When pills became the fashion, he drove to Tijuana, Mexico; bought jars of them; and tripled his money back in Van Nuys.

By nineteen, he had also started using heroin.

He became a steam fitter later and had other jobs, two marriages, and children, but mostly he was, as he put it years later, a "drug merchant." He liked to see himself as sticking it to the Establishment, living outside the law. He bought houses for his family, his kids. Mostly, though, money was used for buying dope, though a good supply was always a challenge. About the only other thing that held his interest was gambling on NFL games.

The Man also served several prison terms. It was during one, in 1993 in Nevada, that he became friends with a man from Nayarit. The Nayarit had come to the United States illegally at eighteen to work *derecho*—"the right way"—and for a time had picked apples in Washington State. Then he made his way to the San Fernando Valley, where he learned the heroin trade and was caught and convicted for transporting cocaine.

As the two shared meals and time together, the new friend told the Man about how the Xalisco Boys had built their unique heroin tienditas, first in the Los Angeles area and then in Honolulu, Phoenix, and Portland.

The Man could help them, he said. The Nayarit's family spoke no English and didn't understand the addict world. So they missed markets and opportunities. But the Man was bilingual and American, and he knew how addicts think. The Nayarit had an enticing pitch: he promised to make the Man rich like you wouldn't believe. And, he could supply him with all the dope he wanted.

They talked about Western markets—Reno, Nevada; Denver, Colorado; Salt Lake City, Utah; and Hawaii. But not all western states—the Man wasn't interested in Texas or Arizona because he had spent too long in California prisons, where Latino inmates from those states feuded with others.

After the Man and the Nayarit got out of prison in 1993, the partners started their first heroin store in Reno. Then they quickly expanded to Salt Lake City.

Later that year, the Man made his first trip to Nayarit, one of the smallest of Mexico's thirty-one states, with a population of less than one million. He fell for the place, returning regularly and buying a half-built home in 1996. He finished it and added on; he took up with a woman, who moved in. She wanted him to spend more time there.

By now, he was managing heroin stores in five cities. He started to grow tired of the many details of retailing: keeping the kids working hard and not straying into partying; replacing a seized car in Denver or a driver arrested in Portland. He began to think about going out on his own.

As he thought about his options, he recalled a card dealer he had met in a Reno casino. Daniel and his wife were longtime heroin users from Columbus, Ohio.

Daniel loved black tar heroin. In Columbus, any heroin they could get was weak powder, heavily diluted. An addict had to spend a hundred dollars or more daily just to not get dope sick.

"You should take this out to Columbus, man," he told the Man one day. "You'd become a millionaire. There ain't nothing like this out there."

And, he added, "I got an uncle I could hook you up with."

When you settle into a new city, it helps to have a guide to show you around. That's what addicts did for the Xalisco Boys. In exchange for help getting started in a new area, as well as help with renting apartments, registering cellular phones, and buying cars, the Xalisco Boys supplied junkies with free heroin.

"You get one person to show you around and pass around the [phone] number and it's like bees to a hive," one imprisoned Xalisco Boy said in an interview. "They all know each other. It's like having a scout."

For instance, he said, a female addict in Las Vegas told some of the dealers, "'I know people in Tennessee.' So they went with her to Memphis. It became one of the biggest markets for a while."

The Xalisco bosses only went to towns with large Mexican populations, where the Boys could blend in and where no gang or Mafia controlled the drug trade. Junkies often found them their first customers.

Most important of all—and crucial to the expansion of the Xalisco Boys—was that addicts could navigate America's methadone clinics.

The painkiller known as methadone was synthesized by German scientists in the effort to make Nazi Germany medicinally self-reliant as it prepared for war. The Allies took the patent after the war, and Eli Lilly Company introduced the drug in the United States in 1947. US doctors identified it as a potential aide to heroin addicts.

Dr. Vincent Dole, an addiction specialist at the Rockefeller Institute in New York City, embraced the idea. On methadone, Dole found, addicts did not demand increasing doses. Instead, they were content with the same dose once a day, which could carry them through the next twenty-four hours. Methadone addicts could actually discuss topics unrelated to dope. This was not true of heroin addicts, whom Dole found tediously single-minded in their focus on the drug.

Dole believed addicts could be maintained on methadone indefinitely and still function as normal human beings. In 1970 in New York City, he opened the first methadone clinic for heroin addicts.

Dole believed that rehabilitation was dependent on human relationships—group therapy, 12-step meetings, and the like. But as a last resort for those who defied all efforts to kick the opiate habit, Dole believed, methadone could be a crutch, helping them.

President Richard Nixon permitted methadone as a treatment for heroin addiction, which plagued many soldiers returning from the

Vietnam War. By the late 1970s, federally regulated methadone clinics were popping up around the country.

Methadone allowed an addict to find a job and repair damaged relationships. There were also no dirty needles, no crime, and addicts knew they couldn't be robbed at the clinics.

Methadone clinics opened before sunrise so that addicts could get to jobs like construction work and carpentry on time. Methadone users were like ghosts, showing up early in the morning for years on end, drinking their dose, and silently going about their lives.

Methadone was often dispensed in small doses, as if the goal was kicking the habit. But as methadone clinics became for-profit affairs, many cut the counseling and therapy that might help patients kick opiates altogether.

The result was that many methadone clinics across the country maintained core populations of opiate addicts on doses that were too small, and usually without much therapeutic support. Addicts who weren't given big enough doses craved another opiate later in the afternoon, after the clinics closed. They usually found their dope on the street, and thus remained tied to the heroin underworld. Some addicts took to using methadone and heroin interchangeably. That made them easy prey for someone with a more efficient and convenient opiate delivery system.

In the mid-1990s, that's exactly what the Xalisco Boys brought to towns across America. They discovered that methadone clinics were, in effect, recruiting stations. Every new cell learned to find the methadone clinic and give away free samples to the addicts.

One Xalisco Boy in Portland told authorities about training that his cell put new drivers through. They were taught, he said, to lurk near methadone clinics, spot an addict, and follow him. They'd tap him on the shoulder and ask for directions somewhere. Then they'd spit out a few balloons. Along with the balloons, they'd give the addict a piece of paper with a phone number on it.

"Call us if we can help you out."

Some of the junkie guides became legend. In Cincinnati, a young woman in the Lower Price Hill neighborhood had been rustling up business for a series of Xalisco dealers for years. Xalisco Boys who were just getting started in Cincinnati asked for her, looked her up, and pushed dope in her face, wanting her help in establishing heroin routes throughout the Cincinnati metro area. It made kicking the habit almost impossible.

"They can't even say my name. But they tell them down there, 'Ask somebody for White Girl. Lower Price Hill.' One guy even came with a note with my name on it. Somebody had written my name and misspelled it," she said. "Over these years, I get out [of jail or rehab] and they're there looking for me. People will say, 'How do you always got this connection?' I don't know. It's not like I call Mexico and say can you send me a guy? But it's always there."

One prolific addict turned guide was a woman named Tracy Jefferson, a longtime drug user from Salem, Oregon. She hooked up with Luis Padilla-Peña, a Xalisco dealer in Reno, Nevada, in 1993. Over the next two years, she helped Padilla-Peña and his family carve out heroin markets in Salem, Denver, Seattle, Colorado Springs, Oklahoma City, and Omaha, Nebraska—usually by enrolling herself in methadone clinics and giving away free black tar to the clinic's clients.

In 1998, the Man was ready for a new challenge. He had spent six months kicking back in Xalisco and making new contacts. In the plaza, parents whose sons he had hired came up to him and shook his hand. One even gave him a pig, another a cow.

He also had a potential guide in the Midwest: Daniel, that card dealer in Reno, had given him the telephone number for his uncle Chuckie in Columbus, Ohio.

"Call him," Daniel said. "He'll help hook you up with everyone you need."

The Man looked at a map and saw three cities in a row: Indianapolis, Dayton, and Columbus. He figured he would try his luck.

On June 11, 1998, he flew into Indianapolis and found a cheap motel off Washington Street, just in time to see his first tornado.

That afternoon, the sky got dark and wind attacked, blowing the rain sideways. Then a massive dark funnel a quarter-mile wide, roaring like a jet plane, came right down Washington Street. He watched it rip roofing off a Pizza Hut and shred a day-care center. A man parked his car and scurried his family indoors. A moment later, the car was gone. They found it three blocks away.

It wasn't the best of omens.

The next day, the Man bought a used car—a brown Cadillac Cimarron for $2,000.

Camping out in front of the town's methadone clinic, he gave away samples of his dope and soon had a client list of desperate junkies avid for the black tar they'd never seen before. Then one day, cops stopped him after seeing a couple exiting his Cimarron near the clinic.

"We've got reports you've been dealing heroin."

"Check the car," he replied. "I got no drugs. I was just dropping them off"—he nodded in the couple's direction—"'cause they needed a ride."

The cops found nothing. But they told him, "We have a photograph of you and your car. Every time we see you, we're stopping you."

So he moved on to Dayton, with a kid he brought in from his Reno store. They hooked up with a dealer, a retired black man, who seemed to know every addict in town. Sure enough, no one in Ohio had seen this kind of dope.

Remembering Daniel's message and the promise of Columbus, the Man drove to the state capital after just a couple of weeks in Dayton. He found a motel and called Chuckie.

They met at the town's methadone clinic the next morning. The clinic was a hive of illegal dope trading. Almost anything a user wanted was for sale. He gave Chuckie a few free samples and his beeper number.

That afternoon, Chuckie called.

"That's some killer stuff you got," he said. "I gotta whole buncha people want some of that."

The Man drove back to Dayton and pulled up stakes.

"We were selling a lot," he said. But his racism against blacks got the best of him. "The thing I didn't like in Dayton was we were dealing with a lot of blacks," whom he didn't trust, he said.

Columbus had more white people, it appeared, and a large community of Mexicans in which to mingle. And shortly, it would have a finely tuned heroin sales machine, the first major city east of the Mississippi River to have one. The Man's timing couldn't have been better: illicit use of the two-year-old pharmaceutical OxyContin was just beginning to create a vast new market for heroin among white people with money.

COLUMBUS, OHIO

Until the Man arrived, Columbus had been a pill town.

Pills were easier to trust than the heroin available there, which had been cut so many times by middle men that it was at most 3 percent pure. It was sold on exactly one street corner. And it was still hard to get.

"Addicts would buy a hundred-dollar bag twice a day just to get well" from withdrawal symptoms, the Man said. "They'd buy a forty-dollar bag of mine and stay well all day."

In many ways, Columbus was ideally situated. Unlike other parts of Ohio, Columbus had sizable immigrant groups—from Mexico, Somalia, Nepal, and other parts of Asia—who flocked to town to fill the low-end service jobs. A large college-student population at Ohio State and other schools has kept it vibrant and edgy.

A metro area of close to two million, Columbus didn't have any organized Mafias or armed gangs controlling the drug underworld, like Cleveland did. It was connected by freeways to regional markets as far east as Wheeling, West Virginia, and south to Lexington and eastern

Kentucky. There was Cincinnati to the southwest. Plus all around it were suburbs and farm towns with money.

The Man immediately sent for two more kids from Xalisco—so now he had three. He brought out a woman from California who rented two apartments in her name: one for the workers and one for him.

He found a car lot with a cooperative owner. Every two months he switched cars. He exchanged an old Honda Accord for a Prelude and that for a Civic and then for a Camry—white, beige, gray. He ran two shifts of drivers: eight a.m. to three p.m. and three p.m. to nine p.m. They devised codes for places to meet the addicts: 1 was a Burger King, 2 a Kmart parking lot.

He tutored his new Xalisco Boys. Never leave the house with anything in your pockets. Take only what you can swallow if you get pulled over. And never carry a gun. An illegal who is arrested gets deported; an illegal with a gun gets ten years.

Some of them still dressed as they had back home, with cowboy boots and belt buckles. "Go to the stores downtown," he told two of them one day. "Look at how they dress the mannequins at JCPenneys. Buy clothes like that so you blend in with the people here."

He insisted they send money home weekly. Some religiously sent money to Mom via Western Union. For some kids, he sent the money to their parents' house himself.

Columbus had the only methadone clinic for hundreds of miles around. As word spread of the high quality of black tar, these pilgrims became some of his first clients—users from Zanesville, Toledo, Chillicothe, from northern Kentucky and western West Virginia. Some of his best clients were buyers from Ashland, Kentucky, who went back home and sold their purchases for triple what they'd paid.

Black tar became the talk of Columbus's drug underworld. "They broke this city down into 'Domino's: thirty minutes or less,'" one veteran addict told me. "Then, every time you found them somebody new, it was a free balloon. Usually it was seven balloons for $100. But if you brought them enough people and were spending with them, you could get as many as thirteen balloons for $100."

With addicts transformed into a new sales force, the Man soon had to concentrate on getting cash back to Mexico. He formed a network of young women. A tailor in Los Angeles made them corsets with pockets that held $100,000 in cash. He sent the women on airplanes to El Paso, where they crossed over the border to Ciudad Juárez and from there back to Xalisco. For more than a year, he sent two girls a month back to Mexico with $100,000 in Columbus, Ohio, profit tucked in their corsets.

His product was coming in from a man named Oscar Hernandez-Garcia, a member of the Tejeda clan who operated a heroin supply business out of his apartment in Panorama City in Los Angeles. Hernandez-Garcia, known as *Mosca* ("Fly"), supplied black tar to Xalisco cells from Portland and Phoenix to Columbus and Hawaii.

The Man used FedEx to move the product from Mosca's apartment in California. He would go to California and buy a small electric oven from Target or Kmart, open the back of the oven, stuff it with tar heroin, then take it to FedEx for packaging. Police didn't often search a package that FedEx prepared. He sent the ovens to a Columbus addict who lived in the basement of his senile parents' home, and he paid him in heroin.

With Columbus humming along, he looked for new markets.

One addict, a kid named Mikey, told him people in Wheeling,

West Virginia, would go crazy for black tar. Mikey introduced him around Wheeling.

There, the Man made a startling discovery. A woman in her late thirties that Mikey knew showed him a bottle of pills, wanting to trade them for his tar for her heroin addiction. OxyContin, the pills were called, she said. He'd never heard the name and initially turned her down.

On reflection, he realized that she drove a new Dodge Durango and owned a house. He'd never known a longtime heroin addict who had a house and new SUV. She told him that OxyContin contained a pharmaceutical opiate, a prescription painkiller similar to heroin. She traveled the area buying these pills cheaply from seniors and then sold them to Oxy addicts in the hills of Appalachia. She bought her daily heroin with the money.

The Man had stumbled into a region where opiate addiction was exploding. By his own good fortune, less than a hundred miles due south was Portsmouth, Ohio, where scandalous pain clinics were starting to follow the lead of Dr. David Procter, providing prescriptions for millions of these pills to long lines of addicts. Meanwhile, specialists were urging well-meaning doctors everywhere to prescribe opiate painkillers for pain.

Central Ohio, in other words, was about to be a great place to be a heroin dealer.

Jeremy Wilder was a tall, lanky union carpenter from Aberdeen, Ohio, about fifty miles west of Portsmouth, who made extra money buying pills from pill mill doctors in northern Kentucky and reselling them in his county. By the mid-1990s, he was the biggest pill dealer in

Aberdeen, while still working carpentry jobs in southern Ohio. Users literally beat a path to a window in his house.

At first, Wilder didn't use the drugs he sold. But one night at a party he broke down and snorted an Oxy. Soon, he was selling to support his habit.

Then, in Cincinnati one day, he couldn't find Oxys. A neighbor of his Cincinnati connection could get something else: black tar heroin. Jeremy initially balked, but the next day, he couldn't take the dope sick anymore. After trying black tar heroin, Jeremy never took the pills again.

For the next two years, he drove daily to Cincinnati to buy pills from a woman and his tar from the Mexicans. He sold the pills to pay for the heroin he used. For a while each balloon he bought from the Mexicans came with a paper attached and a phone number. Call anytime.

In late 1998, Wilder was among the first in southern Ohio to make the transition from OxyContin to heroin. Later, many others would advance from snorting Oxys to injecting them as their tolerance built. But Oxy was expensive on the street and as many reached their financial limits, they switched to heroin. The black tar was potent and far cheaper, and the delivery system made it easier to get than the pills. Plus tar could be smoked—it didn't have to be injected.

The way the Man saw it, every Oxy addict was a tar junkie in waiting, and there were thousands of new Oxy addicts. All he had to do was work it.

Wheeling, West Virginia, taught the Man that new markets were now everywhere the pills were. He found a place in Carnegie, Pennsylvania, a suburb of Pittsburgh, close enough to service other towns like Steubenville and Wheeling.

He also eyed Nashville. Its Mexican population was growing, nearing eighty thousand people. The town, he heard, was swamped in Oxy-Contin. He set up one of his Columbus drivers, along with a new kid from Xalisco, in a store that was soon booming. The Nashville tiendita covered his expenses for a bigger expansion.

At the urging of another addict, he took a trip down to Virginia, through Roanoke, Richmond, and Newport News. It was another large market, but the federal government had too many military installations there. He went through Chattanooga, Tennessee, a town with a lively underworld—but too small.

He drove down to Pensacola and Jacksonville but left. "Florida is dominated by Colombians and Cubans and Puerto Ricans," he said. "Kill, kill, kill—they think they can solve everything by killing. I wasn't gonna kill nobody over drugs."

He nixed Philadelphia, too. It had a huge heroin market, but it was run by the Mafia and street gangs. He didn't even consider New York or Baltimore. It was crazy to think that a bunch of Mexican farm boys could break in there. Plus, the country was full of towns like Columbus—wealthy places with growing numbers of addicts and no competition.

He tried to keep his eastern tienditas a secret from his Nayarit friends. But in a small town like Xalisco, people talked. After a year in Columbus, his drivers went home for the Feria del Elote and started bragging about the great heroin market they were working up in central Ohio.

By the fall of 1999, two more crews were in Columbus. One belonged to a former driver, now venturing out on his own. Two more followed. The price of heroin in Columbus fell.

Competition, as always, attuned the Xalisco crews to customer service. One woman lived twenty-five miles outside Columbus and at one point she hadn't called to buy for three days. A Xalisco Boy called her.

"Señorita, why haven't you been buying recently?"

"I don't have any money," she said.

He drove out to deliver fifty dollars' worth of heroin to her, for which he required no payment. No, it's free, he said.

"He wanted to keep me using, and buying from him," she said. She did both.

A year or so after the Man opened up Columbus, he drove to Charlotte looking for bigger profits at the suggestion of addicted customers.

Heroin, in fact, had only a small market in Charlotte. The Man met junkie contacts at the town's methadone clinic and gave them free samples. Soon, business boomed again. He pulled a driver out of Columbus and another out of Nashville and they set up the black tar heroin franchise in Charlotte.

A couple of weeks later, the Sánchez family, from ranchos near Xalisco, arrived in Charlotte with an addict guide of their own. The Man didn't know them, only knew of them.

It was bound to happen. It was a free market, after all.

NEW MEXICO

One hot day in the summer of 1999, Enrique took a cab to the Yuma (Arizona) International Airport to fly to Santa Fe, New Mexico.

Also in the airport, waiting for a plane, were a dozen Mexican men. Short and brown, they wore dusty baseball caps, jeans, and faded T-shirts. He figured them for illegals, maybe construction workers, proud of their capacity for hard work but without much else on their side. Enrique saw something of himself in those men at the Yuma airport.

Though he had grown up dirt poor, he now had a business, with employees and expenses. Heroin had taken him a long way from the Toad. His false US ID allowed him to cross the border posing as another man, Alejandro Something.

As he waited for his plane, he watched an immigration officer in the airport ask the men for identification. There was some discussion. Then, as the other passengers watched, the officer led them off single file to be, Enrique assumed, deported.

Scenes like this convinced Enrique that he was doing what he had to do to survive. As the officer paraded the men by, he thought to himself, "I'm the dirtiest of them all and they don't ask me anything. If I'd have come to work derecho—honestly—they'd have treated me badly, too."

Watching *la migra* roust those dusty immigrants from the Yuma airport helped put an end to the last nagging qualms he had about selling chiva.

Two years earlier, Enrique had arrived in Albuquerque, intending to start his first heroin business. But soon after, he met an addict from Santa Fe who said construction workers in that city an hour to the north were heavily addicted. He paid the guy $5,000 for introductions to some addicts. He found Santa Fe wide open and quickly set up the heroin cell that had been his goal for almost half his life by then.

He brought in kids from his village. Right off, that felt good—to be an employer, a benefactor. He taught them how to drive, how to package heroin in balloons. He taught them the streets. He paid them $600 a week, plus all expenses, including the coyote's fee to cross them into the United States. Soon his cell was flourishing.

He employed almost two dozen kids over the next three years, from the poorest ranchos. They worked hard, didn't steal, and were grateful. He knew how much was riding on their work—a truck, a piece of land, a girl, the threat of many years in prison.

He spent much of his time in Nayarit. He hired a maid for his mother. He paid for a sister's quinceañera—the traditional Mexican coming-out birthday party for a fifteen-year-old girl. He took his family to fine restaurants in Tepic where they nervously rubbed elbows with the city's middle class.

"At least I'm not going to die wanting to know what's on the other side," he told himself.

Enrique bought the land where he and his father were born. He hired men to help his father in the field.

Seeing his son with some cocaine one day, his father took Enrique aside. Don't use it, he told his son. He admitted he had been a drunk for too long. It was the first time he had spoken to Enrique as a father should to his son.

"That's all fine," Enrique said. "But why didn't you speak to me like this before?"

His father said nothing.

"You have to change," he upbraided his father. "No more yelling."

Rancho fathers didn't speak to their children but instead resolved every problem with blows or orders. Heroin changed that in Enrique's house.

Still, there were headaches at work. Enrique was constantly having to set up apartments for his guys in Santa Fe and get them new cell phones. When a cop stopped one of his drivers, that car was useless.

Finding new workers wasn't that hard; many men knocked on his door back home, asking for work. But making sure they were trust-worthy, then getting them up north and trained—that was a chore, and costly, too. He was always returning to Santa Fe to supervise, make changes, corral his workers, and get them straight. But the business was growing.

From Santa Fe, he discovered a huge heroin market in tiny Chi-mayo, twenty-five miles north. The town, a popular tourist attraction, had fewer than four thousand people. It was known for its cherry-red heirloom chiles and a devotion to tricked-out lowriders, as well as the Santuario de Chimayo, a small adobe church built in 1816. The

church is surrounded by milk-chocolate soil that is said to have heal-
ing powers.

Chimayo also has the highest rate of heroin addiction in America.
For decades, three family clans operated virtual convenience stores,
selling weak heroin to fifty to a hundred addicts a day. Addiction was
almost a culture, something passed down through generations.

But after Enrique's arrival, black tar replaced the diluted heroin.
Burglaries increased. Needles were everywhere. And people began to
die: 2 percent of the population—eighty-five people, many of them
veteran addicts—died of black tar heroin overdoses over the next three
years.

As the death toll rose in 1998 and 1999, families of dead addicts,
joined by priests from a New Mexico order known as Los Hermanos
Penitentes, began protest processions through the mountains to the
santuario. They bore signs with the names of people who had died
from overdoses or been killed by burglars.

Law enforcement began to pay closer attention. Jim Kuykendall, a
longtime DEA agent, was based in Albuquerque after stints in Beau-
mont, Texas, and Bogotá, Colombia. He began to build a bigger case
that went beyond drug sales.

"The key to the case are the bodies," Kuykendall said. "There's a
story behind who these people are, where they bought their drugs, and
how they died. We need to tell that story."

He got the medical examiners' reports of dozens of overdose cases
and realized that addicts, even those well into adulthood, often returned
to live with their parents once they lost their jobs, houses, and spouses.

These parents, it turned out, were eager to talk. They greeted the investigators with tears and hugs; they recounted watching helplessly as their kids fell apart. One mother, crying, pinched Kuykendall's cheeks as she made him promise he would get the people who sold her child heroin.

One afternoon, Kuykendall went to visit Dennis Smith, a man in his seventies whose son, Donald, had died. Donald Smith had moved back to live with his father after a fight with his girlfriend over his heroin use.

The elder Smith said that on the trip home from an outing one night, his son had demanded they return to Chimayo so he could buy heroin. He threatened to jump from the car if his father didn't turn around. Dennis Smith said he drove his son back to the Barelas' family compound. The next morning, he found his son's corpse in the trailer in the back of his property.

George Roybal told detectives that he often took his disabled brother, Ernie, to buy dope from the Barelas and the Martinezes. Another, Lynette Salazar, told them she took her son, Armando, to a clan house, as she had done often, to trade auto supplies for a hit of dope, and from this Armando died later that day.

Kuykendall flew to Montana to visit a woman who had driven through the valley one fall. Enchanted with its natural beauty, she decided to stay. She moved in right next to a member of the Martinez clan.

At first, she told Kuykendall, she believed her next-door neighbor Jesse "Donuts" Martinez was a Boy Scout leader from all the youths who would visit the house in the afternoon. Soon, though, she saw kids with belts around their arms. Her young son began finding syringes in the yard. She called the cops and began noting every car that pulled up—thirty a day sometimes. She spent a year watching addicts coming in and out, shooting up in the backyard in full view of her window. She called police repeatedly; finally, she gave up and moved.

In April 1999, as Kuykendall and others sifted through the Chimayo stories, a twenty-one-year-old Mexican man was killed in Santa Fe. Aurelio Rodriguez-Zepeda, from Xalisco, was found in the trunk of a car, beaten and bloody.

Xalisco meant nothing to the agents at the time, nor was the man's murder especially intriguing. But the car in which Rodriguez-Zepeda was found was registered to Josefa Gallegos, the heroin matriarch of Chimayo. And, as it happened, they found the young man's cell phone.

Numbers in the phone connected to a heroin case that the FBI was investigating in Phoenix. Kuykendall called the FBI in Phoenix and learned that drug traffickers from Nayarit had set up retail heroin cells across the United States in mid-major towns. Nayarits were going to towns like Boise, Salt Lake, Omaha, Denver, Pittsburgh, even Billings, Montana.

In combing phone records for the heroin clans of Chimayo, Kuykendall realized that when clans wanted to order supplies they called a central number—apparently a dispatcher. This dispatcher, the records show, then called Aurelio Rodriguez-Zepeda. The dead person appeared to be some kind of black tar deliveryman for the Chimayo dealers.

Ultimately, thirty-four people were indicted for heroin-related crimes in Chimayo. In September 1999, a long caravan of law enforcement officers rolled into Chimayo as three helicopters buzzed like dragonflies across the skies. Land and lowriders were seized. Ultimately, the long-running Chimayo heroin operation was shut down. But as Kuykendall would soon learn, shutting down the Xalisco Boys would be much harder.

OPERATION TAR PIT

In January 2000, a hundred federal agents and police officers from twenty-two cities gathered at the DEA office in Los Angeles.

Paul "Rock" Stone came in from Portland. Jim Kuykendall came in from Albuquerque. Others came in from Hawaii, Denver, Utah, Phoenix, and elsewhere. Each of their investigations into black tar heroin had once seemed separate, as if heroin dealers had independently sprouted in Maui or Denver.

But in 1999, Los Angeles DEA agents had received information that a heroin dealer in San Diego was getting their supply from a couple in the Panorama City district of the San Fernando Valley. Agents obtained a warrant for the Panorama City couple's phone records.

Oscar Hernandez-Garcia and his wife, Marina Lopez, were from Xalisco, it turned out. He was calling numbers all over the United States from that apartment. With a wiretap, agents heard him arranging shipments of black tar, usually packed into the innards of electric ovens. Among the people Hernandez-Garcia spoke to frequently was the Man, who needed product for his stores in Columbus, Nashville, Wheeling, and Charlotte. Occasionally, the Man, speaking English, followed up with FedEx on packages that had gone missing.

That gathering made graphically clear the national scope of the Xalisco Boys for the first time. An agent from each city got up and described the local investigation, what each was seeing. It was the same story over and over: Drivers would spend a few months driving around with mouths full of balloons. They were caught with only small amounts of drugs and thus were usually deported without even doing much jail time. The cells practiced just-in-time supplying, like a global corporation. They presumed that anyone asking to buy more than a few grams was a cop.

Oscar Hernandez-Garcia supplied them all, and many others, from that Panorama City apartment. He had brothers who were veteran heroin cookers down in Xalisco and kept him stocked.

"It was eerie how uniform [the stories] were from town to town," said Rock Stone. "You couldn't help but feel how corporate these guys are, how standardized they are. It's like McDonald's, where you get the same burger in Louisiana as you get in California."

Yet no single person called the shots. Hernandez-Garcia may have supplied them all, but that didn't mean he gave orders. Nor were their profits funneled to him. He was just a wholesaler; they were retailers relentlessly focused on the bottom line.

Together, the agents and officers hoped to shut them down once and for all.

"You're cheating on me, you bastard," Marina Lopez yelled into the phone at Hernandez-Garcia in Mexico.

Here she was in that run-down apartment, packaging dope all day. Her husband was philandering in their hometown of Xalisco, and Marina was hearing the gossip all the way up in Panorama City.

The argument escalated.

"That's it, woman!" Hernandez-Garcia yelled into the phone. "I'm not coming back. I'm staying down here."

Unbeknownst to the couple, narcotics agents were listening in. The marital spat sent jolts across the country to the highest levels of American law enforcement.

It was June 12, 2000. By now, the case dubbed Operation Tar Pit reached across more of the United States than any other drug investigation in the country's history. The bust was set to take place in three days.

Officials at the US Department of Justice in Washington, coordinating dozens of law enforcement agencies across the country, had set the June 15 bust date weeks before. They were counting on Oscar Hernandez-Garcia being in the US. And now it appeared that a marital tiff was going to keep him in Mexico, which might forever put him out of reach of US justice.

Lisa Feldman, the federal prosecutor in charge of the case in Los Angeles, got on the phone to officials in Washington. "We can't change the date," she was told.

"But he's my lead defendant," she explained.

"We've got too many resources committed. Sorry. It's gotta happen then."

For the next three days, Feldman and the agents waited on edge to see whether Oscar and Marina would make up.

They did.

Oscar Hernandez-Garcia returned to Los Angeles and Lopez. Hours later, a SWAT team hit their apartment. They found dope in the dishwasher and money in a container of baby formula. At the same time, federal agents and local cops swarmed into apartments in Cleveland and Columbus, in Salt Lake City and Phoenix, and in Maui, Hawaii.

In Portland that morning, 108 officers met in a cavernous conference room at a north Portland hotel to discuss how they would hit eighteen residences and another fifteen cars. Rock Stone stayed up most of the night, listening to Xalisco Boys' wiretaps, fearing he would miss something. By then, he had tracked these Nayarits to twenty-seven cities in twenty-two states.

At six a.m. in southwest Albuquerque, Jim Kuykendall and other agents burst into a two-story adobe-style house where Enrique then lived with a girlfriend and her children. They arrested another half dozen of his drivers.

Later, Kuykendall talked with Enrique. "He just portrayed himself as a poor guy from small-town Mexico trying to make a buck—as if there was nothing too wrong with what he was doing," Kuykendall remembered. "A family guy looking out for his family and his kids. I'd talked to too many of the girls he'd slept with to believe that. He was a farm boy . . . and a midlevel trafficker."

Enrique spent the next thirteen years in a US federal prison.

Across the country that day, 182 people were arrested in a dozen cities. Agents seized sixty pounds of heroin and $200,000 dollars, relatively small amounts. Yet Tar Pit remains the largest case—geographically and in terms of manpower—the DEA and FBI have ever mounted jointly. "This is the first time we've seen a criminal drug-trafficking organization go coast-to-coast, also hitting Alaska and Hawaii," DEA administrator Donnie R. Marshall said at a press conference.

The bust reflected the spread of Mexican immigration. Though the traffickers were just a tiny fraction of Mexicans in the US, Mexican immigrants were just about everywhere, and they had many more places to blend in.

The Xalisco Boys succeeded because they were the internet of dope: a network of cells with no one in charge of them all, with drivers rotating in and out, complementing each other as they competed for every user's last twenty bucks, yet doing this without guns and shutting down at any hint of law enforcement's approach.

Back in Xalisco that August, the Feria del Elote was dead. Bandas came to town and left empty-handed. Most cell owners left for Guadalajara, believing they were on some DEA or FBI list. The Man went on the lam, returning to Xalisco just before the feria. "The town dried up," he said.

He was arrested in South Carolina two years later and sent to prison.

In Portland, Rock Stone came to a sobering conclusion. It wasn't just that the Xalisco runners were endlessly replaced. The crew managers were replaced quickly, too. He'd never seen this in narcotics. Informants told him the Tejeda–Sánchez clans alone were more than two hundred deep back in Nayarit, and any of them could rotate into a heroin crew in Portland as a regional sales manager or cell supervisor.

The Xalisco Boys' networks coughed and sputtered but did not die. The cell owners remained in Mexico and reconstituted their US operations. Experienced drivers started their own cells. Wholesale suppliers multiplied in the vacuum left when Oscar Hernandez-Garcia and his wife went to jail. Competition lowered prices and expanded the supply of tar heroin headed to the United States. The next year, the Feria del Elote was bursting with traffickers and bandas once again.

In Santa Fe, a longtime addict remembered that after Tar Pit, there was no dope on the streets—for exactly one day.

PART 3

A New Dreamland

GROUND ZERO

Dr. Peter Rogers, an adolescent medicine specialist, was at home in Columbus one evening in February 2003 when a nurse called with a crisis.

A sixteen-year-old girl was in the Nationwide Children's Hospital emergency room with her parents. She was shivering and throwing up. It was heroin withdrawal, her parents said. The nurses didn't know what to do.

Rogers was doubtful. Tall, thin, and spectacled, he had specialized in addiction for almost twenty years by then. He had treated kids on cocaine and crack. He'd seen them on meth, scratching scabs and grinding their teeth. He'd seen them on ecstasy, LSD, and pot and as full-blown alcoholics. But he had never seen a teenager addicted to heroin.

He drove in, not sure what he would do if he was wrong.

The girl was small and blond and looked like a cheerleader. But she had track marks up her arms. Her face was pale and worn. She had diarrhea and pains in her legs, stomach, and back.

"She said she'd started with pain pills she got from her friends. The pills got a little expensive," Rogers remembered.

Her boyfriend was a heroin user, and he injected her with heroin for the first time. "She used for a while, then she'd run out of money," Rogers said. "Her parents realized something was really wrong. She told them."

Two months earlier, Rogers had taken a course in Cleveland in how to detoxify people addicted to opiates. Unsure what to do, he called the doctor who taught the course.

"He said he had not seen any adolescents using heroin, but he gave me some ideas. I plugged her into an IV, hydrated her, gave her something for her nausea. I learned a lot from her."

The girl was from the wealthy suburb of Powell, which surprised Rogers almost as much as learning that she was only sixteen. "Where do you get your heroin?" he asked.

"From Mexicans."

"Where do you find them?"

She named a neighborhood that white girls from Powell did not frequent.

Rogers kept her in the hospital for three days. Once she had admitted she was a heroin addict and was detoxed, her parents believed she was fine and could go home. Rogers had a different view, one learned from years as a recovering alcoholic himself.

If she doesn't get long-term treatment, she is not going to stay sober, he told the parents. She's going to die, end up in jail, or become a chronic underachiever.

"They didn't believe me," Rogers said. "A few months later, the parents called. They said she's using heroin again. I saw her again, re-admitted her. I think they were getting the message."

After that first patient, however, it seemed like floodgates opened. Rogers watched as a new opiate epidemic seemingly emerged from nowhere and filed through his clinic.

In the early 2000s, all the changes that had been brewing for several years seemed to collide. Roughly drawn, the region with Columbus to the north and parts of West Virginia and eastern Kentucky to the south became ground zero for an opiate epidemic that followed elsewhere in the country.

The American pain revolution was complete: most of the country's one hundred million chronic-pain patients were now receiving opiate painkillers, and doctors believed virtually none of them would grow addicted. Pills were prescribed for wisdom teeth extraction, carpal tunnel syndrome, and severe headaches. Football and hockey players were given them for separated shoulders. People were sent home with ninety Vicodin or sixty OxyContin pills. In many cases, such as patients recovering from surgery, a half dozen pills might have sufficed, but doctors often wanted to avoid additional patient visits.

With so many pills in so many hands, a 2004 survey by the US Substance Abuse and Mental Health Services Administration found that 2.4 million people twelve years or older had used a prescription pain reliever for recreational reasons for the first time within the previous year. That was more than the estimated number using marijuana for the first time. The pain-pill abuser's average age? Twenty-two.

The Xalisco Boys saw their market begin to expand exponentially. A younger and much larger population of heroin users was emerging. The Man had picked his new markets well.

In the past, heroin had appealed mostly to rebellious kids from a seedy urban corner of America's counterculture. "I remember at eleven and twelve years old seeing pictures of [Sex Pistols bass player] Sid Vicious and thinking he's the coolest," one twenty-six-year-old recovering addict, a musician, said. "It was punk and jazz that made heroin so sexy and appealing, exciting and dangerous and subversive and not the norm."

Then the users changed. "I saw the football players and the cheerleaders getting into it," the musician said. "These are people I turned to heroin to get away from."

In the months following the girl's emergency room stay, hundreds of young people came to Children's and Rogers, all of them white, suburban kids from well-to-do homes. Most were girls. One was a tennis champ. Another was the daughter of a Columbus cop. One was the daughter of a thoracic surgeon—several were children of doctors, in fact.

"We were not ready for this," Rogers said. "It was a whole new phenomenon."

All had started with pills. Many said they'd seen friends die. They had no idea where else to go. "I noticed that we got a lot of kids during that first six months from a place called Lancaster," a Columbus suburb, Rogers said. "It turns out these kids were coming to Columbus, buying heroin, going back to Lancaster."

To the suburban kids hooked first on pills, heroin gave them adventures they'd never had in their quiet towns. Part of heroin's appeal was that it kept them at the edge of a hazardous yet alluring new dreamland of both getting a high and maintaining it. Finding dope could take them on a wild ride through worlds they hadn't known existed, which, however scuzzy or harrowing, left them with fantastical stories that awed their peers.

"You're as much addicted to going and buying it as to going and using it," one young addict said. "You feel like James Bond. It's a crazy fantasy."

The trappings of prosperous suburban life helped. Many suburban kids had their own bedrooms. That privilege could also be an addict's sanctuary, the shrine to the self-involvement dope provokes. It was their own little domain, quite the opposite of Portsmouth's legendary Dreamland community pool, where kids grew up in public under a hundred watchful eyes.

"We lived in our bedroom," said one woman in recovery. "You could have a big, huge house, but you could lock that door, isolated. Everybody I ever got high with, it was always in their bedroom."

Most of the kids also had cars, given to them by doting parents so they could navigate pedestrian-proof neighborhoods. Those same cars, intended to take them to school or practice, also were used to meet their dealers—and played right into the Xalisco Boys' business model. In cars, kids shot up, gave rides to fellow addicts, and hid their dope. When their parents' trust in them finally died, the kids lived in these cars, and the cars became their private bedrooms.

By the end of 2003, Nationwide Children's Hospital, which previously had never admitted a teenage heroin addict that anyone could remember, had protocols for treating them.

Rogers called Columbus police to tell them about the Mexicans selling dope. An officer told him they knew all about the young men. They are arrested, and in a day or two, another comes in and takes their place, the officer told him.

Meanwhile, Rogers said, "I was living at the hospital." He called other hospitals around the country and couldn't find another facing the same challenges. Still, the kids kept coming in.

Rogers battled insurance companies, which had apparently never heard of treating heroin addiction in teenagers. A couple of years in, he gave a speech at the annual meeting of the American Academy of Pediatrics in Boston, describing what he was seeing to a sparse and bewildered audience.

"They weren't seeing any of this," he said. "They were thinking, 'Why do we need to learn about this?'"

IMPORTING PILLS

As OxyContin grew in popularity, pill mills like the ones that inundated Portsmouth in OxyContin and Vicodin were popping up all over the country by the 2000s.

Kentucky had tried to rein in the business with a new prescription monitoring system just as the last century was ending. Pharmacies were now required to file reports every two weeks, listing the narcotics prescriptions they had filled and the patients' information. The goal was to identify both heavy prescribers and patients who were going from doctor to doctor for drugs.

Kentucky drug users began searching for new sources of pills for their hometowns.

In spring 2003, Jarrett Withrow joined a crew of ironworkers from Greenup County, Kentucky, just south of Portsmouth, on a job in Fort Walton Beach, in the Florida Panhandle.

Withrow had already given up a lot for dope. He had hoped for a college basketball scholarship but got hooked on Vicodin in high school. He stole OxyContin from his father, who was dying of cancer, and remained addicted to the powerful pills.

Within a couple of weeks on the job, the crews' pill supply began to run short. One afternoon, one of the crew left and came back that night. "Look what I got," he said, holding up bottles of pills he was prescribed that afternoon.

Turned out, Florida doctors were awfully easygoing when it came to prescribing pills.

The Greenup crew began going to these doctors and also asking coworkers from Florida to go and then sell them their pills. The crew members sent the pills back to Kentucky and sold them for triple what they paid.

Even as coworkers hiked what they charged for the pills, "that triggered the idea that this was easy," Withrow said. One friend continued to go to Florida long after the job ended.

"He started telling other people," Withrow remembered. "We was carrying the prescription pill epidemic."

With pain pills now so easily prescribed, opiate addicts spread information on where to find pills the way a cough spreads germs.

Importing was almost part of the culture in Kentucky. Bootlegging alcohol from legal counties into dry areas like Floyd County (pop. 30,000), on the east side of the state, had been common since Prohibition started in Kentucky in 1919.

Timmy Wayne Hall had grown up on Branham Creek Holler in Floyd County, the son of a factory worker who was also a preacher in the Church of God. Hall wasn't interested in becoming a coal miner and managed to never work at a regular job. In 1980, he married into a family of bootleggers.

He began driving down to Perry County, buying cheap beer and selling it out of the family's house in Floyd County for triple his cost. That work dried up after Floyd County finally went wet in 1983, and he looked to the government for support. Hall was prescribed Lorcet after a car accident, which he could afford with his Medicaid insurance card. He grew addicted to the pills, moving up to Oxy later.

With the pills hard to get in Kentucky, Hall found an Oxy connection through a friend in Detroit, Michigan, about four hundred miles to the north. He also found connections in Dayton and Toledo, Ohio, which were more or less on the way to Michigan. He began regularly bringing in pills, and Oxy got a bigger following in Floyd County.

In 2004, a local trucker spotted billboards for a clinic called Urgent Care Services in the town of Slidell, Louisiana. He stopped in, was prescribed a bunch of pills, brought them home, and sold them. He began driving down to Slidell—a seventeen-hour trip—with several Floyd County addicts, bankrolling their visits, then keeping half the pills they were prescribed.

When that trucker died, one of his regulars—who had briefly been a deputy sheriff—continued driving down to Urgent Care Services with addicts, paying for their trips and $500 doctor visits. In payment, he took half the pills they had been prescribed, using some and selling the rest.

Soon dozens of Floyd County folks were making the trek to Slidell. The clinic's owner, Michael Leman, sensing opportunity, opened another one in Philadelphia. Despite the Urgent Care Services name, the clinic had no equipment to treat people with urgent medical needs, such as X-ray machines. The Kentuckians were charged $500 per visit, while locals paid only $250. Then Leman opened an Urgent Care Services even closer, in Cincinnati. Carloads from Floyd County began making pilgrimages to Philadelphia and to Cincinnati each week.

From these Urgent Care Services clinics, a new flood of pills washed into Floyd County.

Hall was among the biggest customers of Leman's new Urgent Care Services clinic in Philadelphia. He traveled constantly back and forth, paying others to drive for him because he was heavily addicted. "I was taking twenty, twenty-five people a month to Philadelphia," he said. "I'd go in there and get their scripts." The pharmacy that filled them was just a few steps away.

With each patient receiving close to five hundred pills at a time, and Hall taking half of that, he was clearing more than $4,000 for every person he hauled up to an Urgent Care Services. He was also scoring pills from Detroit and connections in three other states—though never in Kentucky, as he feared the state's prescription-monitoring program.

Back home, he made a killing on the first day of the month, when the government support checks arrived in Floyd County.

He began hiring dealers to sell for him. At his peak, he figured he had dealers selling in five counties in eastern Kentucky. When he heard of competitors, he would go to their customers and offer them Oxy 80 mg pills for $65 apiece instead of the $70 the competitors were charging. He sold all over, watching as OxyContin seeped into every corner of eastern Kentucky. Men with professional jobs in wealthy Pike County were his pill customers; so were the construction guys who worked on their houses.

With his windfall, Hall bought a dozen houses in and near Branham Creek Holler. He often took friends on road trips and paid for every-one's hotel room. A coterie of addicts hung around him, and he paid them to cook, wash his clothes, vacuum his house, cut the grass, and do odd jobs on his properties. He grew intoxicated with the power—and had a habit of up to twenty OxyContin 80s a day.

Hall was arrested in 2007. During withdrawal, he went into a seizure and was briefly pronounced dead, then spent six months learning to walk again. When he pleaded guilty, Hall confessed to selling two hundred thousand OxyContin and methadone pills, though the real figure was likely far higher.

"I'm sorry for the things I done," Hall said in an interview from federal prison. "I was brought up in the church and didn't want to hurt no one. But I was an out-of-control drug addict who didn't realize who I was hurting."

As one dealer was shut down, another popped up. Soon, Floyd County addicts were headed to Florida, where the Greenup County men had been so successful a few years earlier, and others joined them. Campers voyaged weekly down from the Oxy-wracked regions of Ohio, Kentucky, and West Virginia for doctor visits. Flights from Huntington, West Virginia, to Fort Lauderdale, Florida, were dubbed the OxyContin Express.

By 2009, nine of the top ten oxycodone-prescribing counties in America were in Florida. The other was Scioto County, Ohio, where Portsmouth is located. By the time Florida put in a prescription-monitoring system that year, customers from as far away as Colorado were pill shopping there.

BLACK GOLD

Purdue branded OxyContin as the simple solution for chronic-pain patients. The Xalisco Boys branded their system as the safe and reliable delivery of balloons containing heroin of standardized weight and potency. The addict's convenient everyday solution.

The widespread prescribing of OxyContin and other drugs tenderized pill abusers to heroin. As OxyContin abuse spread, so did the Nayarit trafficking. "They went and took over the OxyContin Belt in America," said one police officer.

Like Purdue, but quite unlike traditional heroin dealers, the Xalisco Boys didn't sit around waiting for customers to come to them. They targeted new ones using enticements and price breaks. They followed up sales to good clients with phone calls that amounted to customer satisfaction surveys. Was the dope good? Was the driver polite?

Drivers would travel across town to sell a $15 balloon. Addicts learned to play one crew off another. "The other guy was giving me seven balloons for a hundred dollars; you're only giving me six." The effect was to keep the addict not only using but also drumming up more customers to get bigger discounts.

Meanwhile Xalisco dealers were constantly monitoring good customers for signs that any of them were trying to quit. Those addicts got a phone call, then a driver plying them with free dope. One Albuquerque addict recalled that he told his Xalisco dealer, whom he considered his friend, he was going into rehab.

Good idea, the dealer said. This stuff's killing you. An hour later the dealer was at the addict's door with free heroin. Now that you're quitting, the dealer said, here's a going-away present to say thanks for your business.

The addict kept using.

A woman in Columbus said her dealer welcomed her home from jail with a care package of several balloons of black tar heroin to get her using again.

For women addicts, in particular, hardened by daily exposure to the worst of human nature, the courtesy and seeming kindness of the young men could be touching. They were farm boys, not thugs or cartel killers. They were polite, raised among the conservative traditions of the Mexican small town, and awed by America—and also American girls. Because they worked so much, often the only girls they met were their customers.

"Every single guy I encountered, they were personable guys," said Kim Ellis, a former addict from Portland. "Once I was in the car, I no longer saw them as people who were making money helping me with my demise. They were just people."

Empathy for her Xalisco dealers made it doubly difficult for Ellis to quit heroin, which she did years later. "In order to kick [it], I had to hate them. If I held on to one thing that was good, even if it was twisted good, I'd hold on to heroin," she said. "They're real people trying to survive in their car and they're meeting others, like me, who are trying to survive in their addiction. Even now, as much as I hate heroin, I don't hate those guys who were my dealers."

In 2005, a patrol officer in the Nashville suburb of Murfreesboro came across an off-duty juvenile-court bailiff smoking a black, sticky substance—heroin. With the help of the accused bailiff eager to reduce his charges, Murfreesboro police put together a few buys and encountered young Mexican sellers. The case expanded and made its way to the DEA.

Harry Sommers had worked on the huge Tar Pit bust as a DEA supervisor in Washington, DC. Now he was in charge of the agency's office in Nashville, and seeing the Xalisco Boys six years later was like déjà vu.

"We had not stopped them," he said. "These guys were moving into new territory."

By the 2000s, these ranchero farm boys, from a county of just forty-five thousand people in a state most Americans couldn't find on a map, had become the most prolific single confederation of heroin traffickers in the United States. They aggressively sought new markets while supplying dope in at least seventeen states, including places where heroin was all but unknown before they showed up.

They weren't the country's only heroin dealers, of course. Detroit, Baltimore, Philadelphia, and New York had drug gangs that had controlled the trade for years. Nor were they the only Mexicans trafficking in black tar heroin. Northern California was controlled by traffickers from the Tierra Caliente, a humid and notoriously violent part of west-central Mexico. Sinaloans, from a state north of Nayarit that was the birthplace of Mexican drug trafficking, controlled the Chicago and Atlanta markets, both of which were major distribution hubs.

Xalisco Boys avoided those places in favor of midsize metro areas like Nashville, Tennessee, and Charleston, South Carolina, that had legions of new young customers and no worrisome gangs. Still, Tar Pit and other busts had changed the Xalisco model. Before, traffickers had recruited only family and extended family members. But as many drivers went to jail, Xalisco bosses brought in workers from families they were not related to.

Mario, an illegal immigrant who had worked for several years as a mechanic in Portland, had agreed to try the business after some financial setbacks. He moved to Columbus to become a dispatcher.

His new boss had some tough advice for him: forget you have children. "Forget that people may do to your kids what you're doing to the children of others," the boss told him during a restaurant meeting. "Otherwise you won't sleep."

"And," the boss added, "don't let the clients die. Care for them. They're giving you money."

Mario earned $500 a week as a dispatcher, taking telephone orders from a roster of users. The network's sales grew to more than $2,000 a day.

Mario hated needles, but he lived far from the effects of what he was selling. "I never saw anyone inject himself," he said. "I never saw people get sick from lack of dope. I never knew how people got sick. I never knew anything of the people who died. Had I known, I'd have left it."

He dispatched drivers around Columbus for four months, until the day the police barged in and he went to prison.

A driver who went by the name Pedro said he began to think of going north to the United States when a heroin trafficker he knew in his village built a house with an automatic garage door. Old people stood in amazement and watched it open and close. He saw other drivers return to town and buy beer for everyone in the plaza. Girls flocked to them. Without land or prospects, he signed up, too.

"Anyone with desire to go up and try his luck could do it," he said.

To most of ranchero Mexico, including Pedro's mother and father, chiva was a disgusting thing. "When my brother went up north, my mother was saying I don't know how you can sell that garbage," Pedro said. "But when she saw the money, she was very happy."

At home, Pedro seemed destined for dead-end jobs. Ultimately, he said years later, "I was tired of work that led nowhere."

When he got a call from a cell boss, Pedro hoped to earn enough to return and open a bakery. The boss sent him and another young man to the border and paid for them to cross with a group of migrants. The other kid was headed to Minneapolis to sell. Pedro was sent to Columbus, and from there his boss sent him to another city that was deemed virgin territory.

The kids Pedro sold to were all white, always ready to try out their high school Spanish: "*Hola, amigo. Como estas? Me gusta mucho la cerveza.*"

Pedro and his coworkers found a furnished apartment. He made a thousand dollars for a few weeks of work. Then he was arrested and convicted of trafficking.

In some ways, US prison offered more opportunity than Nayarit.

Pedro studied for his GED, an alternative to a high school diploma, and was paid twenty-five cents an hour for his effort. He passed. He also worked as a prison landscaper and cook, making twenty-three dollars a month. It was enough to buy a television, a radio, and his own food.

By the time he was released after a few years he had made $900—almost what he had made selling heroin.

He was sent to El Paso, where an officer took him to the bridge leading to Ciudad Juárez and told him to start walking. "Don't come back," the officer said.

A month later, back home, Pedro received a letter from the prison. It contained a check for $430, the remainder of what he was owed for working and studying for his GED.

The investigation that started near Nashville grew to fifteen cities in eight states and became known as Operation Black Gold Rush.

The focus was on the Sánchez family, which had started in the San Fernando Valley in the 1980s, spread to Las Vegas, and landed in Memphis in the early 1990s. In 2004, a Memphis junkie led the Sánchezes to Myrtle Beach, South Carolina. From there, they expanded to Columbia and Charleston and eventually controlled much of the heroin trade in South Carolina.

After finishing a prison term in South Carolina in 2003, Javier "Chito" Sánchez-Torres ended up in Nashville.

A trafficker who worked with Sánchez-Torres said that by the early 2000s, the Sánchezes were well aware of OxyContin's role in the business. "It was part of the marketing strategy," he said. "Chiva is the same as OxyContin; just OxyContin is legal. OxyContin users change to chiva. They can get our stuff more easily than going to a doctor for the pills."

In time, authorities grew to believe that Sánchez-Torres's uncle, Alberto Sánchez-Covarrubias—or Uncle Beto, as he was known—was a major source of heroin in the United States. Sánchez-Torres spoke often by cell phone with his uncle, who gave him frequent instructions on new markets, on when the next supply was arriving, and on managing drivers.

Uncle Beto's networks, and those of his family, were believed to include roughly a dozen cities, plus most of the state of South Carolina. Police in Myrtle Beach had tried six times to dismantle the Sánchez heroin cell, only to see it return each time.

On the day of Operation Black Gold Rush, a year after the arrest of the junkie bailiff in Nashville, hundreds of officers fanned out across fifteen US cities, gathering up Sánchez clan heroin crews: 138 people in all, drivers, telephone operators, suppliers, as well as numerous local addicts.

That day, federal court looked like a hospital ward. Junkies were throwing up, sweating, and falling off their benches.

"If we didn't arrest them they were going to die," said Dennis Mabry, an investigator with the Nashville DEA task force.

Doctors were rushed to court. Several addicts had their arraignment postponed because they weren't fit to understand the judge.

Like Operation Tar Pit six years before, Black Gold Rush showed the vast expanse of the Xalisco system—in this case operated by just one extended family. Nashville was connected to Ohio, North and South Carolina, Indiana, Kentucky, and several states out west.

Alberto Sánchez-Covarrubias—Uncle Beto—was indicted but remained in Mexico, possibly Guadalajara.

As happened after Operation Tar Pit, the Sánchez heroin cells quickly reconstituted.

CORPORATE CRIMES

By 2006, John Brownlee's investigation into Purdue Pharma, the maker of OxyContin, was four years old and finally nearing its conclusion.

The US attorney's office in western Virginia had issued hundreds of subpoenas, scanned stacks of documents into a database, and interviewed dozens of people. The case was being handled in the small Abingdon, Virginia, office, near Kentucky and West Virginia, a coal-mining region where hundreds of people had died of OxyContin overdoses. Prosecutors there had come to believe that the company had knowingly promoted OxyContin as virtually nonaddictive—even though it was clearly very addictive.

Despite its insistent advertising, Purdue had never provided a study to the FDA that supported its claims.

The company's sales staff said in promotional meetings across the United States that OxyContin's twelve-hour timed-release formula meant that the medicine was released evenly, with fewer peaks and declines in euphoria when compared with immediate-release opiates. To illustrate the claim, OxyContin salespeople displayed convincing graphs showing the purportedly mild peaks and troughs of oxycodone in blood plasma.

This was a crucial point. Intense euphoria followed by an intense crash is what produces the cravings that lead to addiction to opiates. If OxyContin didn't cause these extreme peaks and troughs, then its salespeople could claim that the pills carried less risk of addiction than short-acting opiates.

But federal investigators later said that these graphs were incorrect and "falsely" exaggerated the differences between Oxy and its short-acting competitors.

Purdue "phonied up [those] graphs to show a steady level of oxy-codone in blood plasmas," said Paul Hanly, a New York City plaintiff's attorney, who brought a class-action lawsuit against Purdue on behalf of people who said they had been injured by the drugs. "The true graph shows an incredible spike, then *boom*—you go straight to the bottom."

Purdue supervisors also taught salespeople to tell doctors that patients using up to 60 mg of OxyContin could stop abruptly with-out serious side effects. However, federal investigators found that company officials knew of a 2001 British study of osteoporosis patients who suffered withdrawal symptoms when they stopped using Oxy-Contin. "Even after receiving this information," federal investigators wrote, "supervisors and employees decided not to write up the findings because of a concern that it might 'add to the current negative press'" surrounding OxyContin.

Further, the company taught its sales force that oxycodone was harder to extract, and thus abuse, than other drugs—though the company's own studies showed that wasn't true. In 1995 tests, the company found that 68 percent of the oxycodone could be extracted when the pill was crushed and liquefied and drawn through cotton into a syringe. Addicts interviewed confirmed that it was easier to extract the drug from an OxyContin pill than from other, milder opiate painkillers, such as Vicodin or Lortab, that contained acetaminophen.

However, some of the company's other aggressive marking practices had stopped. Four years earlier, the Pharmaceutical Research and Manufacturers of America, a pharmaceutical trade group, and the US Department of Health and Human Services put out voluntary guidelines on marketing opiate painkillers. They urged companies to cease offering inappropriate travel, meals, and gifts to get doctors to prescribe certain drugs, and to stop paying excessive consulting and research fees to doctors. The guidelines prohibited giving away merchandise not related to health care; OxyContin fishing hats became scarce.

In addition, in 2004, the Accreditation Council for Continuing Medical Education issued new rules prohibiting pharmaceutical company influence on content and speaker selection for continuing medical education programs and limited how grant funding could be used. Drug company funding for the seminars dropped off. Today, a lot of continuing medical education is obtained online, rather than at resorts or during fancy dinners or golf outings.

Those changes would turn out to be too little, too late. By 2006, a decade after OxyContin's debut, 6.1 million people in the United States had abused it—that is, about 2 percent of the population. That might seem like a small number, but the crack epidemic, at its height, involved fewer than half a million users a year nationwide, according to government estimates.

And, as with crack cocaine, the sheer numbers of new opiate addicts by the 2000s were enough to throw hospitals, emergency rooms, jails, courts, rehab centers, and families into turmoil.

To build their case, the Abingdon prosecutors sought to interview Dr. Herschel Jick from Boston University. Jick was frequently cited as an expert source for evidence that opiates weren't addictive. But as with so much of the opiate story, the truth was something different from what people assumed.

Back in 1979, Jick had tapped into a database of hospital patient records that he had built to see whether hospital patients were growing addicted to narcotic painkillers. Years later, he could not remember exactly why this question had occurred to him. "I think it was maybe a newspaper story," he said.

A computer technician compiled the numbers. Figuring others might find it interesting, Jick wrote a paragraph in longhand describing the findings. His secretary typed up a paragraph that said that only four patients had grown addicted out of almost twelve thousand patients treated with opiates while in a hospital before 1979.

There was no data about how often, how long, or at what dose these patients were given opiates, nor about the ailments the drugs treated. The paragraph simply cited the numbers and made no claim beyond that.

A graduate student named Jane Porter helped with his calculations in some way that Jick could not remember years later. Porter and Jick sent a letter, signed by both of them, to the prestigious *New England Journal of Medicine*. In its January 10, 1980, issue, the *Journal* published their paragraph on page 123, alongside other letters from researchers and physicians from around the country. The article bore the headline, "Addiction Rare in Patients Treated with Narcotics."

Jane Porter left the hospital, and Jick lost track of her. He turned his attention to other subjects.

But sometime later, "Porter and Jick" were cited in research papers as making a significant claim: fewer than 1 percent of patients treated with narcotics developed addictions to them, they supposedly found.

That "fewer than 1 percent" statistic stuck. But a crucial point was lost: Jick's database consisted of *hospitalized* patients from years when opiates were strictly controlled and overseen by doctors. These were not chronic-pain patients going home with bottles of pain pills.

Others began citing its purported conclusion. That single paragraph was mentioned, lectured on, and cited until it emerged transformed into, in the words of one textbook, a "landmark report" that "did much to counteract" fears of addiction in pain patients treated with opiates.

Purdue would latch on to it as the basis of its claim that OxyContin wasn't addictive. Other studies were cited as well, but it appears that none was mentioned, nor misinterpreted, as often as Porter and Jick's was.

So in 2005, the Abingdon prosecutors sent a subpoena to Jick. He ignored it.

Then a federal prosecutor called, explaining that they needed him to testify to a grand jury about a drug company using his 1980 letter to the *New England Journal of Medicine* as proof that their drugs weren't addictive.

He had no idea what she was talking about. "I told them I wouldn't go," he said later. "But they threatened to put me in jail, so I schlepped on down there. They had me on the stand asking me irrelevant and obtuse questions for two hours."

John Brownlee's case against Purdue proceeded. In 2006, he filed criminal charges against the pharmaceutical company and set October 25 as a deadline for Purdue to accept a plea agreement.

Then, late at night on October 24, he received a phone call at home from Michael J. Elston, who worked in the US Department of Justice in Washington. Elston said he was calling on behalf of a Purdue Pharma executive.

Later, in testimony before the US Senate Judiciary Committee, Brownlee said Elston asked him to slow the case and postpone the plea agreement. Elston later said he was calling on behalf of a superior, who in turn had received a call from a Purdue defense attorney asking for more time.

Brownlee thought about the request. It was a delicate matter, especially since he had some political ambitions at the time. But he didn't see any reason to postpone the long and complicated case. Just that afternoon he had received approval from DOJ higher-ups to proceed with it. He said he told Elston to "go away."

Brownlee signed the plea agreement with Purdue the next morning. Purdue Pharma pleaded guilty to a felony count of "misbranding" OxyContin, and three top executives each pleaded guilty to a single misdemeanor of misbranding the drug.

Eight days later, his name showed up on a list compiled by Elston of federal prosecutors recommended to be fired.

Nine were fired, and in the end, John Brownlee was not one of them. But, he testified the next year, he believed his inclusion on the list was retaliation for not delaying the Purdue settlement.

Elston later resigned. An attorney for Elston told the *Washington Post* later that there was no connection between the phone call that night and Brownlee's name appearing on the list of prosecutors recommended to be fired. But the Purdue episode lingered amid a Bush administration controversy in which top attorney general officials were accused of political meddling in the work of their far-flung prosecutors and recommending some be fired for not complying with seemingly political orders.

Later, when Purdue was asked for interviews about the criminal case, a company spokesman offered only this statement:

"For more than 30 years, Purdue Pharma has developed opioid medications to alleviate the debilitating pain experienced by millions of people. As leaders in our field, we are acutely aware of the public health risks that can arise from the misuse and abuse of these medications. We're working with policymakers and health care professionals throughout the country to reduce the risks involving opioids, without compromising the medical care of people suffering from chronic pain.

"Purdue is developing innovative technologies to create pain medicines in new forms that include abuse-deterrent properties, making them unattractive to drug abusers. These medicines are designed to provide patients with pain relief when taken as directed, while also deterring abuse by snorting and injection. These new approaches do not prevent abuse, but they are a step in the right direction.

"We encourage a transition to abuse-deterrent technologies over time, but it must be accompanied by greater societal efforts to reduce the demand for non-medical use of prescription medications."

In fact, the company did reformulate OxyContin pills so they couldn't be snorted or injected—but not until 2010.

In July 2007, Purdue executives appeared in federal court for their formal sentencing. To avoid federal prison sentences for its executives, the company agreed to pay a $634.5 million fine. Three executives— Chief Executive Officer Michael Friedman, General Counsel Howard Udell, and the by-then-departed chief medical officer, Dr. Paul Goldenheim—paid $34.5 million themselves. They were also placed on probation for three years and each was ordered to perform four hundred hours of community service.

During the proceedings, Lee Nuss, the mother of a Florida man who died of an OxyContin overdose, rose to speak.

"You are," she told them, "nothing more than a large corporate drug cartel."

TIDAL WAVE

Even as prosecutors were pressing criminal charges against Purdue, the full impact of the OxyContin explosion was still unfolding.

In Washington State, Jaymie Mai and Gary Franklin from the Labor and Industries Department had looked to Jennifer Sabel, the state's epidemiologist, to see if the whole state was seeing a spike in deaths like they were among workers injured on the job.

Sabel and her team pulled together all the death certificates and coroner's reports of people who had died from opiates. It was a complicated task that required a coroner's paperwork on each death. But it confirmed what Mai and Franklin had found.

In 2004, 386 people died of opiate overdoses statewide—a sixteenfold increase from twenty-four deaths in 1995.

Worse, a tidal wave was forming ahead. Overdose deaths already far outstripped those during the crack rage in the late 1980s and even those in the mid-1970s, when heroin was last popular. But overdose deaths advanced in lockstep with the amount of opiates prescribed statewide, so the more pills prescribed, the more deaths there would be.

"We couldn't believe the volume, the number of cases," Mai said. "This is a huge problem and it's just going to increase every year unless we do something about it."

But when Sabel stood in front of fourteen of Washington's top pain specialists at a Seattle hotel in December 2005, the room was silent.

This couldn't be true, said one doctor, finally. There must have been some coding error, another said. Death certificates are notoriously unreliable, said a third. Others spoke skeptically of Sabel's data.

Franklin had to jump in to say that the same trend was obvious at Labor and Industries. "I think there's really something here," he told the specialists.

The response, Sabel said later, reflected the doctors' shock at the impact of their prescriptions. "They've been convinced by the drug companies that it's okay to prescribe these medications for people with chronic pain because here's the studies that show very few of them will become addicted," she said. "They don't want to hear that the people they're prescribing these drugs to might die. They're physicians and they're trying to help people."

At the meeting, Labor and Industries proposed a guideline for general practitioners when prescribing these drugs: if doctors had patients taking more than 120 mg a day with no reduction in pain, then they should stop and get a pain specialist's opinion before prescribing higher doses.

It was simple and reasonable enough, but it was contrary to an idea central to the pain revolution: that there was no limit on how much opiate painkiller a patient might be prescribed. The guidelines would make Washington the first state in the country even to suggest some control on how many narcotic pills doctors were prescribing.

The state officials put the question to pain specialists, and, eventually, the doctors came around, suggesting that Labor and Industries put out guidelines for prescribers suggesting limits.

Not surprisingly, two Purdue Pharma executives wrote to object to the idea of a ceiling on opiate doses. "Limiting the access to opioids for people in chronic pain is not the answer," wrote Lally Samuel and Dr. J. David Haddox in the 2007 letter. They were concerned that patients who needed more opiates "may be undertreated while they are waiting for consultations with pain specialists, as required by the guideline."

Not long after, the proposed guidelines got caught up in a legal battle.

While Washington State officials were trying to change narcotics prescribing, an Ohio official was just seeing a new and frightening trend.

Ed Socie was a longtime epidemiologist with Ohio's department of health who tracked data of deaths from violence and injuries. In 2005 he was startled to notice that poisoning deaths in Ohio were climbing, based on data from the federal Centers for Disease Control.

He dug into the numbers. The poisoning deaths, it turned out, were actually drug overdoses. This was new. Cocaine and methamphetamine— the popular drugs through the 1980s and 1990s—are damaging drugs, but people don't often fatally overdose on them. Heroin, which people do overdose on, hadn't been a sustained problem since the 1970s.

Socie graphed these new numbers. After remaining stable for decades, the deaths suddenly took off like an airplane, almost tripling in six years. Looking closer, he saw that opiates were present in virtually all the deaths where the drugs were specified.

The numbers alarmed Socie, and he showed them around his department. But no one seemed to share his concern until Christy Beeghly took over as the injury prevention program administrator in 2007.

Socie showed the new boss his data and charts depicting the sudden increases in fatal drug overdoses, a large number from prescription pills. They dissected the numbers further and came to an astonishing conclusion: drug overdose deaths were about to surpass fatal auto crashes as Ohio's top cause of injury death.

This was a stunning moment in the history of US public health. Since the rise of the automobile in America, vehicle accidents sat atop the list of causes of injury death in every state and in the United States as a whole. By the end of 2007, that was no longer true in Ohio.

Nationwide, drug overdoses passed fatal vehicle accidents for the first time in 2008.

Socie and Beeghly also found a tight relationship between the quantities of prescription painkillers dispensed annually in Ohio and overdose deaths. Both rose more than 300 percent between 1999 and 2008. But even that hid the full truth.

The use of some opiates, like codeine, actually declined. Meanwhile, dispensed grams of oxycodone—the only drug in OxyContin—rose by almost 1,000 percent in Ohio during those years.

They wrote a report, published in 2010, revealing once-camouflaged facts:

- In 2005, Ohio's overdose deaths exceeded those at the height of the state's HIV/AIDS epidemic in the mid-1990s.

- Three times as many people in Ohio died of prescription pill overdoses between 1999 and 2008 as died in the eight peak years of the crack cocaine epidemic.
- The number of Ohioans dead from drug overdoses between 2003 and 2008 was 50 percent higher than the number of US soldiers who died in the entire Iraq War.

In Portsmouth, in the state's southern end, Scioto County coroner Terry Johnson had been tracking drug overdoses for several years. Because his office had a small budget, he sent bodies to medical examiners in larger counties for full autopsies and blood tests. These invariably turned up opiates, usually combined with benzodiazepines—the old Dr. Procter cocktail.

As pill mills sprang up, fatal overdoses increased. He also kept track of what he termed "drug-related deaths"—a death that was probably related to a person's addiction but was officially deemed, say, a heart attack. When he did that, the numbers doubled.

By 2008, Scioto County had twenty-one fatal drug overdoses and twenty-three drug-related deaths—giving it the second-highest death rate in the state. He had tried to bring local doctors, pharmacists, and elected officials together to address the problem, but nothing came of it. Nor did state boards governing doctors and pharmacists try to rein in pill mills.

"No one was looking at it until the state Department of Health realized our numbers exceeded [fatal] traffic accidents," he said.

By then, the tidal wave was gathering strength. Sales of oxycodone were still growing. Abuse of prescription painkillers was behind nearly half a million emergency room visits nationally in 2011. A government survey found that 620,000 people reported using heroin that year, up 66 percent in four years. Most telling: 80 percent of them had used a prescription painkiller first.

Further, US overdose deaths involving opiates rose from ten a day in 1999 to forty-eight by 2012.

In Washington State, the new prescribing guidelines were stalled for two years by the legal fight. Twenty-five workers, each of whom had gone to a doctor with a work injury, died of opiate overdoses in 2008; in 2009, thirty-two more died.

Finally, in May 2011, a judge threw out the troublesome lawsuit. State legislators repealed the intractable pain regulations that protected doctors who prescribed unlimited doses of opiates. And Washington issued the guidelines on prescribing that Franklin and Mai had come up with—the first state to suggest ways for doctors to temper their opiate prescribing.

SILENCE

Not long after the Ohio report was published, Christy Beeghly called Portsmouth city nurse Lisa Roberts. She wanted to set up a meeting with women from around the state to talk about the problem.

Roberts invited a friend and public health colleague. This was finally a chance to talk about the devastation that pills had wreaked along the Ohio River. They drove to Columbus. It was quickly apparent, however, that the other women in the room had no idea about what had hit Portsmouth.

"We're [sitting] there and they're telling stories about how wonderful their daughters are. Each one is, like, 'My daughter's in college; my daughter has a Ph.D.,'" Roberts remembered. "I pass a note to my friend: 'What are we going to do?'

"She passes one back to me: 'I'll tell the truth if you will. These women need a wake-up call.'"

When it was her turn, Roberts told the gathering that her daughter was a pill addict who had stolen from her blind. As a result, she had forced her daughter out of the house.

"My daughter," her colleague said, "is in jail accused of executing three people for their pills." Half of their coworkers' kids were addicted. They followed with a description of the pill mills, of the OxyContin barter economy, of the constant overdose deaths.

The room was silent.

"I remember coming home and being real mad," Roberts said. "It's not right that our kids are having their futures and freedom taken from them because they've fallen prey to this horrible chemical that steals their soul. Our kids shouldn't be going to the grave."

Beeghly put together a presentation on overdoses, with one chart showing a red stain of overdoses spreading north out of southern Ohio. Then-governor Ted Strickland used an emergency executive order to form a state opiate task force to recommend policy changes—the first Ohio-wide effort to address the problem.

Advocates like Lisa Roberts and her friend were extremely rare. Even as tens of thousands of people a year died from opiate overdoses, most grieving families retreated in shame and never said a word publicly about how a son died in a halfway house with a needle in his arm or a daughter overdosed.

It was as if the powerful drugs narcotized public ire as well. That it began in voiceless parts of the country—in Appalachia and rural America—helped keep it quiet at first.

Then, as heroin and OxyContin addiction consumed the children of America's suburban white middle classes, parents hid the truth and fought the scourge alone. Friends and neighbors who knew shunned them.

"When your kid's dying from a brain tumor or leukemia, the whole community shows up," said the mother of two addicts. "They bring casseroles. They pray for you. They send you cards. When your kid's on heroin, you don't hear from anybody, until they die. Then everybody comes and they don't know what to say."

These family members could have been—and in later years would become—some of the most powerful voices for change. But as the number of overdoses and deaths soared, they were largely silent.

This baffled law enforcement, health-care providers, and prosecutors fighting the growing crisis. At the Carolinas Medical Center in Charlotte, North Carolina, Bob Martin was seeing a very different kind of addict. A former New York cop who was now director of the hospital's substance abuse services, he realized that half of CMC's patients addicted to opiates had private health insurance.

He studied the zip codes where they lived and found that they came from the town's wealthiest neighborhoods—Raintree, Quail Hollow, Mint Hill—places with winding streets and garages filled with Jet Skis and shiny SUVs. These areas were also home to nine country clubs and the region's best shopping malls. It was as if the Xalisco Boys had done market research.

This thought also occurred to a Charlotte undercover police officer who went by the name Jaime. He had been working narcotics at the Charlotte Police Department since 2007, buying from Xalisco dealers hundreds of times.

Officers like Jaime and prosecutors had tried to stop the heroin flow. When Sheena Gatehouse rejoined the Mecklenburg County district attorney's office in 2009, black tar heroin dominated the drug caseload. Addicts were overdosing and dying, and Gatehouse's office instituted a new rule: no easy deals on heroin cases.

Prosecutors began winning twenty-year sentences for drivers. But each bust seemed to provide an opening for more crews, so that an arrested crew was replaced by not just another one but sometimes by two. With more dealers on the streets, the price of heroin dropped. Balloons containing a tenth of a gram started at $20 each, then went to $10. Finally, by 2011, you could buy fifteen balloons of potent Xalisco black tar heroin for $100—$6.67 a balloon, about the price of a pack of cigarettes.

One bust in 2012 especially made Gatehouse question the approach. A dozen cops spent months buying from Xalisco drivers. Finally, they busted the drivers and a dispatcher. They also arrested some addicts, seizing their cell phones.

Three days later, those confiscated phones started ringing. Xalisco dealers were calling; the store was back in business with new drivers up from Mexico. Officers hadn't even finished processing the evidence from the bust.

Gatehouse went back and forth on the wisdom of the tough approach. The damage the dealers did clearly required it. But, she said, "we're sending a farm boy away for twenty years and have had no impact."

It would have helped to somehow tame the demand. But as an undercover officer, Jaime saw no outrage in Charlotte. He spoke to the parents of one addict after another. As soon as he said the word "heroin," their minds crashed to a halt. They couldn't conceive of their children on heroin.

For every symptom, the parents had an answer. Did they see burned aluminum foil around the house? We thought he was burning incense.

Was he slurring his speech? He was getting over the flu. Were his grades falling? He was going through a phase.

Jaime spoke to the city's Drug Free Coalition, which was focused on alcohol and marijuana.

"No," he told them. "Heroin is the real problem."

He and Gatehouse spoke to a group of headmasters from Charlotte's best private schools, hoping it would ignite a local crusade. It didn't.

Despite spreading addiction, none of the dozens of parents he spoke to came forward to warn school groups, churches, or the media. Heroin touched the families of doctors, ministers, bank executives, and lawyers, but they retreated from it, crushed by grief and the drug's stigma. This was just not something you talked about at the country club.

A half dozen reporters asked Jaime for contact information of parents who had lost children. He would plead with the parents to come forward and tell their stories to help keep the next kid from dying. None did.

A conspiracy of silence enveloped Charlotte. Heroin continued to seep through the city and neighboring suburbs across the state line in South Carolina.

PART 4

Responding

A NEW APPROACH

For years, law enforcement in Portland, Oregon, would bust Nayarit drivers and then ship them back to Mexico, rather than locking them up in precious jail space. Xalisco traffickers came to believe Portland would go easy on them, and more and more of them flocked to the Rose City.

Finally, tired of failing to dent a growing heroin trade, Portland-area officers took a new approach: they would build Len Bias cases, a strategy named after a superstar college basketball player who was the second player taken in the 1986 National Basketball Association draft. Two days after the Boston Celtics drafted him, Bias tried cocaine with a friend. The drug caused a heart attack that killed him.

A Len Bias case is based on a federal law that imposes a twenty-year prison sentence on the person who supplies drugs that cause a fatal overdose. Officials have to prove the person died from the suspect's drugs. If they can, they have a powerful prosecutorial tool that can take them to higher-ups inside a drug network.

One of the early cases that Portland officials chose was the death of Toviy Sinyayev, a seventeen-year-old high school junior who was the oldest boy in a large Russian Pentecostal family.

In March 2011, Toviy told his mother, Nina, that he had the flu. He went out with his older sister Elina and they returned hours later. He seemed different, but Nina was too busy tending to the younger kids to pay close attention.

The next morning, she found him in bed, unconscious and gasping for breath. Paramedics couldn't revive him. He lasted for three days on life support.

Tom Garrett, one of two detectives in the tiny suburb of Milwaukie, in Clackamas County, found balloons of heroin and a syringe in Toviy's bedroom.

Under pressure, Elina told police that their dealer was a Russian Pentecostal heroin addict named Aleksey Dzyuba.

They put a wire on Elina. Going through withdrawal and with her brother on life support, Elina met Dzyuba in a Safeway parking lot, as a dozen undercover officers watched. She bought heroin from him and passed him some marked cash. As he drove from the parking lot, officers descended and arrested him.

To save himself from a Len Bias prosecution, a dealer needs to flip, and quickly, burning the dealer one link above him in the chain, hoping for leniency at sentencing time. The last man detectives can trace to the drugs faces the twenty years if convicted—a fateful game of musical chairs. Thus, a heart-to-heart takes place in an interrogation room.

Investigators can't threaten a suspect, but they do tell him what he faces under federal law. "The tone in the room definitely changes," Garrett said. "You're not joking with them. It's a very powerful conversation."

Speaking through a Russian interpreter, Dzyuba bridled at this idea. People die every day for their addictions, he told his interrogators. He wasn't to blame for their choices. Finally, though, a defense attorney explained the situation. Dzyuba gave up the name of the dealer he bought from. With that, Garrett and his colleagues began working up the chain.

Dzyuba's dealer gave them the name of his supplier, who in turn gave them his dealer. This dealer, three levels up from Toviy, said he bought daily from a Mexican he knew only as Doriro.

About two decades earlier, tens of thousands of Russian Pentecostals immigrated to the United States in search of religious freedom. In their strict Christian religion, women wore head scarves; dancing, jewelry, and makeup were prohibited. They were pacifists and foreswore guns and television. They married young and had lots of children. Many of them settled in Sacramento, California; Seattle, Washington; and Portland.

Anatoly and Nina Sinyayev, from the city of Baksan, were among them. Anatoly was a welder. Nina's father was an evangelist, touring Germany and Israel to preach the gospel. When the Soviet walls tumbled in the early 1990s, the Sinyayevs took their two toddler daughters and fled to Portland.

Nina's first baby in America was Toviy. The couple had ten more children. Anatoly was always working. They moved eight times, mostly in the Portland suburbs of Gresham and Milwaukie, where Russian Pentecostals concentrated. They attended a conservative Russian Pentecostal church and raised their children in their faith.

But their American dreamland contained hazards they hadn't

imagined. Remaining Christian in America, where everything was permitted, was harder than maintaining the faith in the Soviet Union, where nothing was allowed. Churches were everywhere. But so were distractions and sin: television, sexualized and permissive pop culture, and wealth.

The Sinyayevs' daughters were not allowed to wear nail polish or mingle with Americans. But Anatoly kept a television in the basement and turned it on when he thought his children weren't listening. They watched it when he wasn't home.

As they moved into adolescence, the Sinyayevs' oldest children hid their lives from their parents. Elina, the stubborn second child, applied makeup on the school bus each morning and exchanged her long skirts for pants. After school, she donned Pentecostal clothes, removed her makeup, and arrived home looking as plain as she had when she left.

Elina tried heroin the first time with a friend from work, who told her it would relax her. Her sister started with OxyContin. So did Toviy. Elina lost her job and, desperate for her dope, began dating a Russian Pentecostal heroin dealer, who got his tar from the Mexicans.

Elina believed she was the only one in her family using heroin. But one night at home, she looked at her sister and brother and watched them nod off and knew the truth. Two decades after Anatoly and Nina left the Soviet Union for the freedoms of America, each of their three oldest children was quietly addicted to black tar heroin from Xalisco, Nayarit.

For a Len Bias case to work, federal, state, and local government agencies have to cooperate completely. The state medical examiner has to be willing to quickly perform an autopsy; the local DA has to give up the case if it appears the feds have more leverage.

Above all, investigators have to share information. That's because, unlike traditional Mexican drug organizations, Xalisco cells actually shared supplies, even with competitors. Xalisco cases tended to connect like webs.

While narcotics officers are "creative, innovative, persistent," said Kathleen Bickers, a federal prosecutor with a specialty in Len Bias cases, "they're very territorial. We constantly have to remind ourselves to break those barriers down, to think organizationally, and not just think that 'it's my case.' You are going to go up a couple levels and you're going to run into somebody else's case."

Not all cities are that cooperative or organized. In Denver and elsewhere, officers just kept busting drivers, taking their cars and putting them out of business. At the least, they figured, they were raising the cost of the Xalisco traffickers to do business and taking profits from the drug bosses. In Portland, though, the new approach was winning support.

With Doriro's number in hand, Milwaukie police detective Tom Garrett and his colleagues called his phone. No one answered. They called through the afternoon.

Nothing.

Unbeknownst to them, Doriro, the man who went by Joaquin Segura-Cordero, was at that very moment being arrested by another department. Portland police also were pursuing a Len Bias death case against him. This one originated three hours away, in Bend, Oregon, where a twenty-one-year-old named Jedediah Elliott had overdosed and died a couple of months before.

Both heroin chains led to Segura-Cordero, who, as it turned out, was a kind of regional sales manager for a Xalisco heroin cell. Normally, Segura-Cordero would have been insulated from the kind of day-to-day heroin sales that would expose him to arrest. But Segura-Cordero had faced a classic small-business problem: a labor shortage.

"He had several runners arrested, so he'd run out of runners," said Steve Mygrant, one of the prosecutors in the case. "He was having to expose himself. He was taking calls and making deliveries himself."

The Segura-Cordero case showed that Xalisco heroin spread for 150 miles around Portland. It went out to the quietest rural counties, where kids, addicted to pills, learned to drive to Portland, buy cheap black tar, and triple their money back home while feeding their own habit.

Segura-Cordero was sentenced to fourteen years in prison for selling dope that killed Sinyayev and Elliott.

Following the death of her brother, Elina Sinyayev assured her parents she had cleaned up. But she was actually using more than ever. She was rarely at home, escaping Toviy's memory and her own responsibility in his death.

One night, her father came to her room, knowing something was wrong. They had never understood each other. As he sat down, he took her purse from the chair and heard metal clinking. Inside, he found two heroin spoons.

She expected rage. Instead, his eyes grew teary. For the first time in her life, he pleaded with her.

"Elina, you need help," he said.

Elina broke down and cried, too. That night, rushing back to heroin, she texted a friend and asked for money. The friend texted back, "No, but I know a church. It's different."

A Russian Pentecostal former addict named John Tkach had started a rehabilitation clinic in the Portland suburb of Boring after he saw the Russian Pentecostal churches ignoring hundreds of addicted kids. Parents who asked a pastor's help with their addicted child were shamed as running a sinful house.

Tkach sold his trucking business, took out a second mortgage on his house, and opened his center. A church formed around it, making the opiate addiction of Russian Pentecostal kids the focus of its ministry. God Will Provide, as the new church was called, rested on Jesus's message of love, forgiveness, and transformation. Traditional Russian pastors called it blasphemy and sinful. Russian Pentecostal kids called it the Rehab Church. But soon God Will Provide had spread its church/rehab center model to Sacramento, Seattle, and elsewhere.

There, Elina met Vitaliy Mulyar, who had once fancied himself the largest OxyContin dealer to Russian Pentecostals in Portland. He had become addicted to black tar heroin and been arrested. In 2010, Vitaliy faced a two-year prison term if he failed a probation drug test.

Terrified, he turned to God Will Provide, where he felt warmth in church for the first time. He kicked heroin, became a Bible teacher, and, with a judge's consent, went on a mission to the Ukraine and Austria as the church, fired by the new energy of its recovering-addict congregants, opened a school for missionaries.

A year into his recovery, Vitaliy encountered Elina at the center. He told her his story. She mistrusted her own capacity to change. But it struck her, the way he had risen from the street. A chaste romance followed, in keeping with Russian Pentecostal tradition, though with a modern American twist. They grew acquainted via hundreds of texts while he was on his mission trip. Vitaliy came home and asked Elina to marry him before they ever kissed.

Two years later, their daughter was born. They named her Grace.

TREATMENT

At the same time that law enforcement looked for new ways to crack down on the Xalisco Boys' heroin business, a hardline approach to the crimes of drug addicts began to soften.

Judge Seth Norman, a longtime Nashville criminal court judge, saw the change firsthand, and he knew it wasn't cost savings or a newfound understanding of drug treatment.

Rather, he said, it was about race and class. These people in trouble weren't African American inner-city crack users and dealers. Instead, most of Tennessee's new addicts were white, middle and upper-middle class, and from the state's white rural heartland—people who vote for, donate to, live near, do business with, or are related to the majority of Tennessee legislators.

Norman, who retired in 2018, ran the only drug court in America that is physically attached to a long-term residential treatment center. He took addicts accused of drug-related nonviolent felonies—theft, burglary, possession of stolen property, drug possession—and put them in treatment for as long as two years as an alternative to prison. Down the hall from his old courtroom are dorms with beds for a hundred people—sixty men and forty women.

Now in his eighties, with a head of white hair and a Southern drawl, Norman started the drug court/treatment program in 1996 and built it almost single-handedly by scrounging beds and ovens and lawn mowers from Tennessee state surplus.

Part of his efforts included frequent visits to the state legislature, where his pleas for more funding fell on deaf ears for a good long time. He would try to convince lawmakers that the drug court and long-term treatment could keep most addicts out of prison—saving the state $32,000 a year over what it cost to house an inmate. Only 20 percent of those who finished the court's treatment program relapsed and ended up back in trouble, compared with 60 percent of those leaving prison, he told them.

Before the pill-and-heroin epidemic, many legislators saw drug treatment as soft-headed do-gooderism. They preferred the lock-'em-up attitude of voters in a red state like Tennessee. But the opiate epidemic made a lot of criminal-justice reformers out of rock-ribbed white conservatives, as they saw up close the impact of a criminal record.

Parents were realizing that life with a criminal record was as stunted as life with an opiate addiction. Any dreams these kids' parents once had for them were now improbable. Even qualifying to rent an apartment was hard. With a record, finding a job after the great recession was almost impossible.

"One thing that makes [legislators] more amenable to treatment is that it's hard to find a family now that hasn't been hit by addiction," Norman said. Fifteen years ago, he went on, "very few members of the legislature had them. 'Naw, ain't nobody in my family going to touch anything like that.' Not so anymore. Now they have seen it firsthand."

Norman couldn't have imagined this when he was scrounging surplus sofas and coaxing pennies from elected officials in the late 1990s. To encourage support, he had named several dorms at his treatment facility for friendly legislators—Haynes Hall, Henry Hall, Waters Hall. Now, he said, the governor and state directors of corrections, public safety, and substance abuse all supported his approach.

Republicans across the country seemed to be changing their views. In Texas, Georgia, South Carolina, Ohio, and other states, GOP lawmakers were pushing for what the *Wall Street Journal* termed "a more forgiving and nuanced set of laws."

"You're seeing this huge groundswell for criminal justice reform really being driven by conservative circles," said Chris Deutsch, with the National Association of Drug Court Professionals. "Conservative governors are starting to invest in drug courts. In the last five years, we're really starting to see statewide drug courts in every county."

In Ohio, the opiate epidemic had swollen the prison population beyond capacity. Prison director Gary Mohr, appointed by Governor John Kasich, a Republican, told a newspaper that he favored expanding prison drug treatment—and had done so in four prisons. He also suggested that he would resign if the legislature decided to build more prisons in response to the epidemic.

Texas opened drug courts and was able, therefore, to close prisons. Kentucky congressman Hal Rogers, a staunchly conservative Republican, has become a strong proponent for drug courts since his district, which included Floyd County, has been hammered by prescription pill abuse. "The epidemic of illegal drugs is by far the most devastating thing I have seen in my more than forty years of public service," Rogers said on the front page of his website, where he also touted the thirty drug courts in his twenty-four-county district.

Kentucky state legislator Katie Stine, a Republican, introduced a bill that made it easier to charge a heroin dealer with the death of someone who died from an overdose. But key to Stine's bill was increased funding for addiction treatment and education.

"You used to think, 'Oh, the heroin addicted, that would be someone in some back alley, someone I don't know,'" Stine told a local TV station. "Now . . . it is your kid. It's your next-door neighbor's kid."

Georgia governor Nathan Deal heard recovering addicts tell their stories at graduation ceremonies from the drug court where his son is the presiding judge. "They all have their own stories, but a common thread runs through all of them," Deal told the *Journal*, explaining why he had tripled the number of drug courts in three years. "They were given a second chance, and they had been rehabilitated."

Several factors made this politically feasible in states like Georgia. Declining crime rates were certainly one. Stressed budgets during the great recession were another—though treatment has always been proven cheaper than incarceration.

Yet the fact was that, coincidentally or not, this change of heart was happening among conservatives just as opiate addiction was spreading among both rural and middle-class white kids across the country, though perhaps most notably in the deepest red counties and states.

Firsthand exposure to opiate addiction, apparently, can change a person's mind about a lot of things. Many of their constituents who were enamored with "tough on crime" talk when it involved urban black kids felt differently now that it was their kids who were involved. So a new euphemism was emerging: "smart on crime," allowing these politicians to support the kind of rehabilitation programs that many once had attacked.

UNTREATABLE PAIN

The first news stories about Wes Workman's death in April 2008 said the eighteen-year-old died from a gunshot.

But in the days before he died, while he was still comatose in a hospital, his mother decided she would tell a different story. Jo Anna Krohn pledged to herself to share her son's real history, the one so many other parents had worked to keep secret.

"I was going to be honest," she said a few years later. "I wasn't going to try to hide what had happened. If I said it enough, maybe another family would never be in my place."

That place was one of unspeakable pain.

Living with his father, Wes began smoking pot at thirteen, and at fourteen began using pills at parties. He was handsome, a linebacker known as a ferocious hitter, and popular. So a lot of what he did was forgiven and he got used to that.

By his senior year in 2008, he starred on the field for Portsmouth High School—but he also had a minor criminal record. He was dealing

156

Oxys from his father's house and bought a gun for protection from a convicted felon.

Five weeks before graduation, Wes was high and partying in his father's basement with younger kids. As a lark, Wes put the gun to his head and pulled the trigger. He lingered on life support for thirty-six hours.

Eight hundred people attended his funeral. The family played "Angel" by singer Sarah McLachlan. His death was on the *Daily Times* front page four days running. Five of his organs were donated.

Wes wasn't the first Portsmouth kid to die. McLachlan's song, written in memory of an addict friend whose life slipped away in a "dark, cold hotel," was becoming a standard at youth funerals, the soundtrack to Portsmouth's swelling opiate epidemic. But ashamed families gave other reasons for their losses, and the local newspaper was careful not to reveal too much about these deaths.

A year after Wes's death, a high school invited Krohn to speak. The mother of five and a substitute teacher told the kids the full story of Wes's drug use and addiction. Another high school invited her. She brought photos of Wes to a town meeting, showed them around, and told what there was to tell.

Soon grieving mothers gathered around her. It was like they had been waiting for somebody else to start talking. They put photographs of their dead children on an abandoned building downtown. That finally put faces to the town's unspoken curse. Families of dead kids found the freedom to talk publicly.

In 2010, she formed SOLACE, a group for parents mourning the loss of children to opiates—the first of its kind in Portsmouth.

When Krohn and some mothers appeared at an attorney general's press conference in green SOLACE T-shirts, the media took notice.

Krohn began getting phone calls from other counties and realized that kids were dying all over Ohio. Chapters of SOLACE formed in sixteen counties. She spoke in Brown and Knox counties, up in Chillicothe, in Ironton—everywhere except for the high school Wes attended and that now offered a scholarship in his name. Portsmouth High never invited her.

Though Krohn is no longer involved in SOLACE, her courage in speaking out opened the door for many other parents—but it was challenging. She grew overwhelmed one day, waiting to give a speech with her childhood friend Karrie. They had grown up doing chores and swimming at the local pond and, as teens, sneaking a beer now and then. They double-dated, imagining how they'd marry and raise kids.

Now in their fifties, each woman had lost a son to dope-related gunshots—Karrie's son Kent was murdered in 2000. Each woman also had another son who was strung out. Krohn's oldest lived in a trailer without running water. Karrie's second son had been to prison three times, and she had PTSD from thirteen years of dealing with her two sons' addictions. The women had once found Karrie's son in a fast-food restaurant bathroom, shooting up.

What had become of their girlhood American Dreams? Krohn wondered.

"We used to catch snakes in the creek," she told her friend. "Who would've ever thought that we'd be here together?"

Looking the other way as young people abused pills may have been easier because some of these new addicts were high school athletes—the charismatic golden youth of these towns. Athletes opened the door for other students, who figured that if cool jocks were using pills, how bad could it be?

Medicating injuries so athletes could play through pain was nothing new. But as oxycodone and hydrocodone became the go-to treatment for chronic pain, organized sports—and football in particular—opened a virtual gateway to opiate addiction in many schools.

Carter was the son of a banker and from one of California's wealthiest communities, where he had been a high school star in football and baseball. Playing almost year-round, he battled injuries that never healed. A doctor prescribed Vicodin for him, with no warning on what Vicodin contained or suggestions for how it should be used.

"In my town, the stands were always filled. You wanted to be the hero," he said. "I taught myself to not pay attention to any injuries."

Most athletes on Carter's teams used pills for injury or recreation. Soon Carter grew addicted to Vicodin and then to OxyContin. He was caught selling pills but told not to do it again. As a student athlete at a Division I university, he began using heroin.

Tyler Campbell, from a Columbus, Ohio, suburb, also played football. He so loved the sport that he walked on as a safety for the University of Akron Zips in 2007 and made the team.

His hard work won Tyler a scholarship for his sophomore year. In the first game of the season, he started against a monstrous Wisconsin team, and for one week, he was the nation's leader in tackles, with eighteen. That was an unusual number for a player in the secondary, highlighting the team's weakness on defense.

Sometime during the season, Tyler injured his shoulder. It never fully healed. He had shoulder surgery after the season ended, and a doctor prescribed sixty Percocets. He was given no instructions about the drug and how to use it. His parents were sidelined by a snowstorm and unable to be with him as he recovered and began to take the pills.

By the next season, unbeknownst to those close to him, Tyler had transitioned to OxyContin.

In 2009, Akron opened a thirty-thousand-seat football stadium, a monument to corporate America in sports. The $61 million Info-Cision Stadium, named for a company that operates call centers, also has a field named for the Summa Health System, a nonprofit hospital; club seating named for FirstMerit Corporation; and a press box named for a local credit union. If ever the Division I school needed a good year from its team, 2009 was it.

Instead, the team disintegrated under the pressure to win and the weight of pills.

Jeremy Bruce, a wide receiver on the team, said coaches and trainers felt more pressure after a number of players suffered injuries. After the games, some of the trainers produced a large jar and handed out oxycodone and hydrocodone pills—as many as a dozen to each player. Later in the week, a doctor would write players prescriptions for opiate painkillers and send student aides to the pharmacy to fill them.

"I was on pain pills that whole season—hydrocodone or oxycodone. I was given narcotics after every single game and it wasn't recorded. It was like they were handing out candy," Bruce said later.

By the end of the 2009 season, the Akron Zips football team was a poster squad for America's opiate epidemic. The Zips' star quarterback, Chris Jacquemain, grew addicted to OxyContin after suffering a separated shoulder. He began stealing and was expelled from the team early in the 2009 season, then left school. Jacquemain's life spiraled down. He died of a heroin overdose two years later.

As the season wore on, Bruce said, "I would say fifteen to seventeen kids had a problem. It seems that most who had an addiction problem had an extensive problem with injuries as well."

Toward the end of the season, he said, players had learned to hit up teammates who had just had surgery, knowing they would have bottles full of pills. Meanwhile, a dealer from off campus sold to the players, visiting before practice sometimes. He fronted players' pills and was repaid from the monthly rent and food allowance that came with their scholarship.

The 2009 Zips had only three wins. The coaching staff was fired at season's end.

J. D. Brookhart, the team's head coach that year, said he knew nothing of the extent of opiate use on the team that Bruce describes. "That wasn't the case, that we knew of," he said. "I don't think it was anything that anybody thought was anything rampant at all. Not from the level I was at."

Trainers and coaches weren't authorized to provide pills, said Brookhart, who has since retired from coaching. "These pills were ordered by doctors."

During the 2009 season, Tyler played eleven games but made only thirty-one tackles. He grew secretive and distant, which teammates and family attributed to his play on the field. In the spring of 2010, his grades dropping and his behavior moody, Tyler was sent home. Over the next year, he was in rehab twice and relapsed. At some point, he switched to heroin.

In June 2011, his parents checked him into an expensive rehab center in Cleveland. Thirty days later, he drove home with his mother, Christy, clean, optimistic, and wanting to become a counselor. The next morning she found him dead in his bedroom of an overdose of black tar heroin from Columbus—likely hidden in his room from before he entered rehab, his father, Wayne, believes.

Like so many others, Tyler's family had kept his addiction a secret. But when his son died, Wayne told his wife, "Let's open it up. Come out and be honest."

The Campbells had three hundred wristbands made for the funeral: Just Say No for TC. Tyler's obituary urged mourners to donate money to a drug prevention group.

Fifteen hundred people attended the memorial. As they consoled him, Wayne was struck by how many murmured in his ear, "We've got the same problem at home."

Two weeks later, Wayne met with fathers who wanted to do something in his son's memory. He knew few of them but learned that several also had addicted kids. That marked a moment of clarity for Wayne Campbell. "When Tyler died, it lifted the lid," he said. "We thought it was our dirty little secret. I thought he was the only one. Then I realized this is bigger than Tyler."

From that grew a nonprofit called Tyler's Light, which became Wayne Campbell's life's work. He spoke regularly to schools about opiates, showing a video of white middle-class addicts, one of whom was a judge's daughter.

Wayne invited others to join him. Among them was Gary Cameron, commander of the Columbus Police Department's narcotics unit. Cameron's team was fighting the Xalisco heroin networks crawling through Columbus; meanwhile, as he told auditoriums full of school kids, his stepson was addicted to their heroin.

"We were quick to talk about the problems we associated with crack," Cameron said one day, after a Tyler's Light presentation. "We just don't talk about heroin addiction."

In 2012, after Wayne Campbell formed Tyler's Light, Paul Schoonover called. Could he and his wife, Ellen, help in any way? Schoonover asked. It had been a few months since their son Matt had died from a black tar heroin overdose, the day after leaving three weeks of drug treatment.

Their younger son's death had blindsided them. At Matt's funeral, Paul told the hundreds of mourners how Matt had died. About the pill use, the OxyContin, then the heroin. He told them how through all this, Matt seemingly led a normal suburban life—he played tennis and golf.

Matt had goals but had trouble following through to accomplish them. Still, he was working and part of the family. He never dressed shabbily, and though he ran out of cash quickly, he never stole from his parents. His bedroom door was always open. He never looked like what his parents imagined an addict to be. Yet all the while, he led a dual life.

"Was I seeing what I only wanted to see?" said Ellen later. "I might have been."

Shortly after Matt's death, Paul and Ellen Schoonover attended the speech of a motivational speaker with a breakfast group of well-heeled middle-aged couples like themselves. The speaker that day asked them to imagine a second half of their lives about more than just enjoying what they'd accumulated.

"The question was 'How do you take that second half of your life and make something significant from it?'" Paul said later. "Maybe not a lot of people come to that question. I don't know that I would have. We knew what we were going to do."

The Schoonovers took Matt's death as a calling. They once thought addiction was a moral failing and now understood it as a disease. They had thought rehabilitation would fix their son. Now they saw that a relapse was all but inevitable, and that something like two years of treatment and abstinence, followed by a lifetime of 12-step meetings, were needed for recovery.

After kicking opiates, "it takes two years for your dopamine receptors to start working naturally," Paul said. "Nobody told us that. We thought he was fixed because he was coming out of rehab."

Instead, drug abuse creates what Ed Hughes of the Portsmouth Counseling Center called "the fifteen-year-old brain."

Opiates and other drug abuse stunts the part of the brain controlling rational action, making abusers impulsive rather than thoughtful, like, well, fifteen-year-olds. "It's like the drug came in there and overwhelmed that brain chemistry and the front of the brain did not develop," Hughes said. "The front of the brain has to develop through mistakes. But the first reaction of the addicted person is to head back to the family: 'Will you rescue me?' Whatever the person's rescued from, there's no learning.

"Most relapse," he said, "comes not from the craving for the drug. It comes from this whole other level of unmanageability, putting myself in compromising situations, or being dishonest, being lazy."

One reason is that it takes the brain a long time to heal enough from the abuse to make good decisions again—"thirty to ninety days," said Dr. Richard Whitney, an addiction specialist in the wealthy Columbus suburb of Dublin. "Otherwise, it's like putting a cast on a broken bone and expecting someone to run five miles."

Few people get the full treatment they need, instead going in for just three weeks or six weeks. "It's as if we said, you only get half the chemotherapy you need to treat your cancer," he said.

Paul Schoonover said if his family had understood that, "we would never have let Matt alone those first few vulnerable days after rehab."

Instead, he remembered, "we let him go alone that afternoon to Narcotics Anonymous his first day out of rehab. He had his new clothes on. He looked good. He was then going to play golf with his friend. Instead of making a right turn to go to the meeting, he made a left turn and he's buying drugs and dying."

The speaker's question that day prompted the Schoonovers to channel their grief. Both of them began to speak about how Matt died, sharing their story with rehab centers, parent groups, nonprofits, and schools.

"Nobody can do it on their own," Paul said. "But no drug dealer, nor cartel, can stand against families, schools, churches, and communities united together."

Ellen, in particular, felt like she had been included in a national secret about the prevalence of addiction. It soothed her to write occasional letters to Matt and speak to parents with addicted kids on the topic "What I Wish I'd Known." A main point: after three weeks of rehab, no addicted child is "fixed."

"There was so much evil in all of this," she said. "We will turn that into something good. We can embrace it and find meaning from Matt's death."

EVERYWHERE

On Super Bowl Sunday 2014, America awoke to the news that one of its finest actors was dead.

Philip Seymour Hoffman, forty-six, was found that morning in his New York apartment, a syringe in his arm and powder heroin in packets branded with the Ace of Spades near his corpse. Blood tests showed he had heroin in his system, combined with cocaine, amphetamine, and benzodiazepine.

The Oscar-winning actor—a father of three—had checked into rehab the previous May for ten days, and then, pronouncing himself sober again, left to resume a hectic film schedule. Just as the death of Rock Hudson thirty years ago forced the country to recognize AIDS, Hoffman's death awoke it to the opiate epidemic.

Within days, media outlets from coast to coast discovered that thousands of people were dying. Heroin abuse, the news reports insisted, was surging. Almost all the recent heroin addicts were first hooked on prescription painkillers, they reported.

This was not new, however; it had been happening for fifteen years.

Alabama now had heroin. Mississippi and southern Louisiana did, too. Rural towns in Indiana and Oregon were bad. Eastern Idaho, North Dakota, and Wyoming were, too. West Virginia saw fatal heroin overdoses triple in five years; Cabell County, where Huntington is located, had the highest number in 2012, with twenty-six people dying from too much heroin.

Local media from upstate New York and Minneapolis ran large and continuing stories about heroin. The *Albuquerque Journal* reported an 80 percent increase in heroin use in New Mexico. The Ohio River valley and Salt Lake City were swimming in it. Heroin was all over New Hampshire and Vermont, and Vermont governor Peter Shumlin dedicated his entire 2014 state-of-the-state speech to the new plague.

Fast-food restaurants developed a heroin problem. Across the country, people were using their convenient bathrooms as places to shoot up. There, locked in isolation, many overdosed and died. In Boston, the problem got so bad that the city's public health commission asked fast-food workers to do periodic bathroom checks and began training workers to notice the signs of overdose: a person's slowed breathing or lips turning blue.

Heroin had spread to most corners of the country because the rising sea level of opiates flowed there first, ushered in on the prescription pads of physicians, the vast majority of whom were sincere in intent. Drug traffickers only arrived later and took far less profit than did the companies that made the legitimate drugs that started it all. "What started as an OxyContin and prescription drug addiction problem in Vermont has now grown into a full-blown heroin crisis," Governor Shumlin said.

In Simi Valley, California, residents agonized over a spate of opiate overdose deaths—eleven in a year. Simi Valley, conservative and religious, has long been home to many Los Angeles Police Department officers. Simi's vice mayor was a Los Angeles police officer.

For years Simi was one of America's safest towns—and, according to crime statistics, it still is. But with pills everywhere and heroin sold in high schools, its kids were now also dying of dope. Simi youths clogged the methadone clinic. Nearby Thousand Oaks, Moorpark, and Santa Clarita told similar stories.

Low crime and high fatal overdose rates—this was the new American paradigm. A happy surface over an ominous reality.

"We came to this safe city and we're doing everything society's asked us to do and yet here we are burying our kids," said Susan Klimusko, whose son, Austin, died from a heroin overdose.

Other parents found their families stuck in a perpetual nightmare. Barbara Theodosiou, a public relations consultant near Fort Lauderdale, had two sons addicted amid the height of the Florida pill mill boom. Figuring there must be others like her, she started a website—addictsmom.com—and a Facebook page with the motto "Sharing without shame."

By 2014, the page had grown to fourteen thousand mothers, who consoled and prayed for each other as they wrote in the rawest terms about collect calls from jail, $40,000 rehabs, syringes found in sofas, funerals planned, and their kids reaching three hundred days clean. Theodosiou added a page for grandparents raising their addicted kids' children. At times the comments reached the pitch of a primal scream of maternal agony, a kind of mass group therapy for a drug epidemic in the virtual age.

"For 6 long years I've begged, pleaded, screamed, yelled, cried, grounded, took things away, called the police, kicked him out & not to mention the countless hrs feeling guilty & terrified for him," one woman wrote about her heroin-addicted son who had just been thrown out of rehab again for failing a drug test. "And the thousands of dollars spent on rehab, hospital bills & therapist as well as bailing him out of jail. I have prayed prayed prayed & prayed . . ."

Despite the ongoing crisis, plenty had changed in the medical community.

Two decades into the pain revolution, doctors had come to realize that opiates were unhelpful, even risky, for some varieties of chronic pain, including back pain, headaches, and fibromyalgia. One 2007 survey of studies of back pain and opiates found that medication "use disorders" were common among patients, and "aberrant" use behavior occurred in up to 24 percent of the cases. It was unclear, the authors found, whether opiates even had an effect on back pain long term.

In fact, many doctors now seemed to eschew opiate painkillers as energetically as they had embraced them a few years before. However, patients who truly needed low-dose opiate treatment for their pain were having difficulty finding anyone to prescribe it.

In Washington State, the prescribing guidelines that Labor and Industries issued were having a notable impact on what Gary Franklin had called "the worst man-made epidemic in history, made by organized medicine."

By 2012, overdose deaths in the state had dropped to 388 from 512 in 2008. The number of injured workers dying of overdoses had fallen by half from its peak, as had the number of injured workers who had become chronic opiate users.

Purdue Pharma's reformulated OxyContin truly had made it

harder to deconstruct and inject the pills. But there was still a swollen population of OxyContin addicts nationwide. Without access to the old Oxy, they flocked to heroin in even greater numbers.

The pharmaceutical industry's sales force arms race ended. By 2014, the number of pharmaceutical sales reps had fallen to 60,000 from 110,000 in 2005. Purdue cut its sales force in half and then, in 2018, eliminated it altogether.

The FDA was now requiring drug companies to provide patients and doctors with education on addiction risks from timed-release opiate painkillers—a commonsense extension of the patients' rights movement, though one that came inexplicably late.

The FDA, meanwhile, reclassified Vicodin from a Schedule III drug to a more restrictive Schedule II. It also denied approval of a generic timed-release form of oxycodone—a no-name OxyContin. But then it approved Zohydro, a timed-release pill similar to OxyContin, containing as much as 50 mg of hydrocodone per pill, though without acetaminophen or anything else to deter abuse. The agency's own advisory committee of pain specialists recommended against Zohydro and was overruled.

Purdue followed that with an announcement that the company would soon seek FDA approval for its own timed-release hydrocodone pill—though this one would include an abuse deterrent. The FDA approved another Purdue drug, Targiniq ER, which combines timed-release oxycodone with naloxone, the opiate-overdose antidote.

Within a few years of the criminal case brought against the company by John Brownlee's prosecutors in Abingdon, Virginia, *Fortune* reported, Purdue was selling $3.1 billion worth of the drug a year, although that number has since slipped.

After more than a decade in which chronic pain was treated with highly addictive medicine, there still was no attempt to bring the studies of pain and addiction together. Specialists in pain and in addiction might see the same patients, but they didn't attend the same conferences or read the same journals.

The Joint Commission for the Accreditation of Healthcare Organizations was now promoting multidisciplinary approaches to pain, including adopting healthier behaviors, psychological support, and nonopiate medications, along with the education of patients on the addiction risks of opiates. And multidisciplinary pain clinics were seeing a rebirth. Their menu of services had been shown to help many chronic-pain patients over time.

Pain as the fifth vital sign was no longer gospel.

"Opioids are effective pain medication. They do work. But a pill is just not always the answer," said Dr. Gavin West, a top Veterans Health Administration clinician. After years of watching too many vets with chronic pain succumb to addiction, the VHA had opened pain clinics that included physical therapy, acupuncture, massage, and swimming-pool therapy, as well as social workers and psychological counselors to help vets suffering chronic pain find work and housing and resolve marital problems. The VHA has seventy of these clinics around the country. The numbers of high-dose opiate patients have fallen dramatically. The goal was to get patients back on their feet, going to work and their kids' soccer games.

"To do those things, you have to approach the patients holistically. We not only have a financial stake, but an ethical stake in this, too," West said. "We're lucky, though. We have the advantage of taking the long view."

Many medical insurance companies, notably, have not found the same virtue in multidisciplinary care.

Attitudes about addiction treatment and attention to the problem were also changing.

In 2013, Ohio governor John Kasich, a Republican, went around the Republican-dominated legislature and expanded Medicaid health insurance to everyone in the state, which in turn gave thousands of families a way to pay for long periods of outpatient drug treatment.

The next year, Jennifer Miller, chief probation officer in Marion County, Ohio, took another step to address her caseload, which was mostly made up of opiate addicts. She applied for a state grant to try an opiate-blocking drug, Vivitrol. Four months in, Miller had a waiting list for Vivitrol, and some of the county's worst abusers were clean. But each shot cost $1,200, and an addict needed it once a month.

"The million-dollar question," Miller said, is how long addicts will need to be on Vivitrol. So far, no drug company had stepped forward to help defray the cost. However, in Marion County, opiates and the Vivitrol experiment got police, jailers, court officials, and probation officers all working together in ways that hadn't been necessary or common before.

Colleges were also taking note of the need for a different approach to recovery on campus. The movement had begun years ago in response to alcohol and marijuana abuse. Rutgers, Brown, and Texas Tech universities pioneered the movement's hallmarks: dorms free of drugs and alcohol, regular 12-step meetings, counseling, drug-free social events, full scholarships for recovering addicts, and majors in addiction therapy. The movement gained huge momentum and spread to many more schools with the opiate scourge. Ohio State was part of it.

"It's been white middle- and upper-class kids," said Sarah Nerad, a recovering addict from the Houston suburbs who was getting a master's degree at Ohio State. "Their parents are the ones who are going to the schools saying, 'What are you doing for my kid?' It really gets the attention of parents and schools when you have kids heavily addicted to opiates and heroin."

The roster of universities with new recovery movements sounded like the top college football rankings and reflected how dope addiction had swept red states: the Crimson Tide of Alabama and the Bulldogs of Georgia, Ole Miss and Southern Mississippi, Baylor, Texas, Vanderbilt, Tennessee, Virginia—as well as Oregon, Michigan, Michigan State, Penn State, and several smaller schools—all had campus recovery movements in response, largely, to pill and heroin abuse. Ohio State had opened a twenty-eight-room recovery dorm.

Still Ohio's overall problem raged. The Department of Health released numbers for fatal drug overdoses in 2012: a record 1,272 Ohioans had died that year, and, of those, 680 were due to heroin. In one three-month period, fully 11 percent of all Ohioans were prescribed opiates. For all the new approaches in medical practice, public health policy, and treatment, there was still pill addiction, there was still heroin use, and the number of those dying was still growing.

CHANGES

A lot was changing for the Xalisco Boys.

For many years, Xalisco-area families shipped small amounts of black tar heroin to the United States, running under the radar of Mexico's larger and more dangerous drug cartels. A report on local Mexican governments found that Xalisco was the 111th wealthiest of the nation's 2,445 counties.

In 2010, however, the Zetas, a violent cartel operating just to the south of Texas, and the Sinaloa Cartel went to war in southern Sinaloa, near the northern border of Nayarit. The violence spread south and engulfed tiny Xalisco.

The results were predictable. Dead bodies appeared here and there. In one shootout, eleven people were killed, including Jose Luis Estrada, known as El Pepino, "the Cucumber," a reputed local drug boss. Xalisco officials spoke of canceling the Feria del Elote and the State Department warned Americans against traveling to Tepic. Cell leaders, who had already been moving to Guadalajara, moved there at a faster clip; they kept a low profile and couldn't live in the houses they had spent so much heroin money building.

This went on for more than a year until it appeared the Zetas triumphed. Cell leaders began paying protection money to the cartel and things calmed down.

The flow of Xalisco black tar into the cities of America never slowed, however. East of the Mississippi River, Xalisco drivers tormented Nashville, Memphis, Indianapolis, several cities in South Carolina, Cincinnati, Charlotte, and, of course, Columbus, and the suburbs for miles around each city.

In Florence, Kentucky, narcotics officers arrested a cell of Sánchez family operators, including one local woman who had been a go-between for the family in Nashville during Operation Black Gold Rush in 2006. The cell had been using local white drivers to deliver heroin, providing them with cars and cell phones—presumably because it could no longer find laborers back home to do the job.

The Boys remained decentralized, resilient, and adaptable. They embodied America's opiate epidemic: quiet and nonviolent. They focused on new opiate markets and worked in as many as twenty-five states, all via one small county in Mexico.

By 2014, heroin trafficking was expanding dramatically across America, fed by the efficient networks the Boys had created, combined with the aggressive marketing of pain pills. New dealers, many of them addicts, were getting in on the action every day, gnawing at the markets the Xalisco traffickers had been cultivating and finding new ones.

Meanwhile, the potency of brown powder heroin from other regions of Mexico, sold by black gangs out of Detroit and the East Coast, was getting stronger. The Sinaloa Cartel seemed to have massively upped its heroin exports to Chicago, New York City, and elsewhere. Heroin seizures at the US–Mexico border multiplied.

For those who wanted to avoid dealing chiva, an incipient avocado industry was overtaking sugarcane and coffee in Xalisco and providing welcome work for many. Around 2009, growers from the state of Michoacán, Mexico's avocado center, brought money and partnered with local farmers to plant avocado orchards. By 2014, those orchards were bearing fruit.

Many of the young men there had been arrested and served prison terms in the United States for selling heroin. Now with a criminal record, they faced lengthy prison terms if they were caught again up north. So they were turning to work in the area's growing new business.

For all the money that black tar heroin brought into the area, few men from Xalisco seemed substantially better off. Cell owners did well and cars with US license plates were common, bearing plates from California, Ohio, North Carolina, Utah, Colorado, and Oregon. But many of the hundreds—or even thousands—who had gone north remained tied to a cycle of boom or bust, spending money quickly, then having to return to the United States to work some more. In the Landarenas and Tres Puntos neighborhoods, several streets were still unpaved.

The Man was still living in California's Central Valley, but time had taken its toll. His hair was gray, his face was pale, and he was weak with liver problems. As he talked, his body seemed to slowly deflate into his chair.

Little of the drug trade lucre trickled back to the Man anymore. "I don't ask them for nothing," he told me. "I hope they make a lot of money. As long as they acknowledge me when I'm over there. I just want respect. That's all."

He had used the cartel peace in Xalisco to return for Christmas. He saw many of the older guys, some still going, others barely getting by. The onetime black tar wholesaler, Oscar Hernandez-Garcia—Mosca— was back in Xalisco with his wife. He and his brothers were rumored to own the local rodeo arena at the entrance to town.

The Man had seen the Nayarit, his friend from the Nevada prison and partner in his first heroin cells. During the cartel conflicts, masked gunmen broke into the Nayarit's home while he and his family were out and took the television, jewelry, and a lot more. They brought a trailer and made off with prized horses that he often rode in the parade through town.

The Man came back to California. Here in the Central Valley, he was frail and anonymous. None of his neighbors knew the story of the heroin cells of Xalisco, the misery he spread, or the many young men who went to prison. He spoke often of going home for good to Xalisco, his adopted town, but that seemed unlikely. As he talked, he slouched, his speech grew faint and slurred, and his eyelids fell to half-mast.

"You never apologize for what you are. I don't. I did what I did," he said, grazing a palm down his face. "I never intentionally set out to hurt anybody. Payback's a sonofabitch, but, what the hell, you live with it."

Breaking from addiction—and helping others do it—was hard work.

In Columbus, where the Man introduced black tar heroin fifteen years ago, Judge Scott VanDerKarr oversaw a weekly heroin court that tried to help former addicts convicted of crimes get back on track. Each must seek counseling, submit to random drug tests, and attend ninety Narcotics Anonymous meetings in ninety days. After that, they attend his Friday sessions every week for up to two years. At the end, they hope to get their criminal records cleared.

Almost half finished the program. But many relapse; some die.

Demand was so great that VanDerKarr had to divide the sessions into two and extend the hours.

One Friday, VanDerKarr called several clients before him, applauded their days clean, and asked about their job searches and whether they had 12-step sponsors. The former prosecutor considers himself an understanding magistrate. But years in heroin court have also taught him that addicts, like children, need clear limits and consequences.

"What it's taught me is that jail is actually a good thing" for those who relapse, he said one day after court adjourned. "I mean, give them a consequence of a couple weeks or thirty days. A lot of time it takes maybe two of those" to motivate them.

Robert Berardinelli considered himself lucky that he never had to do that. Just the fear of jail time convinced the longtime Santa Fe addict to get clean.

Busted as part of Operation Tar Pit, he felt blessed to have escaped with probation. Now a group leader in Narcotics Anonymous, he said, "I believe in the power of the twelve steps. It's why I'm here right now. It's tailor-made for people like me."

But as black tar continued to be sold in Santa Fe, the area set an overdose record in 2012. The new customers were often young. Narcotics Anonymous had responded by creating special meetings for addicts in their twenties.

Berardinelli vividly remembered the moment fourteen years before when DEA agent Jim Kuykendall and his team rolled up to arrest him.

Their indictment held a dozen Mexican names and his. Berardinelli had put their phone bills and car titles in his name. He was gaunt, pocked, scabbed, and worn-out. He could lie no more.

Kuykendall led him to a patrol car in handcuffs. "This is the first day of the rest of your life," the agent said as he put him in the car.

It took a while, but Berardinelli came to see that as the truth. He was now a grandfather and grateful for his second chance. "Jim Kuykendall saved my life," Berardinelli said. "For years now, I've wanted to just say, 'Hey, man, thank you.'"

PORTSMOUTH

In 2012, a lanky, hollow-eyed man arrived in Portsmouth, Ohio, his arms purple and scraped with needle marks, a third of his teeth gone, and half his life wasted. He carried with him $10, a couple of Percocets, and a few sheets of scrawled poetry he had written.

The thirty-five-year-old addict Jeremy Wilder was escaping his life in Aberdeen, an hour to the west. His entire adult life had coincided with the opiate epidemic and the decline of small towns like his own. He spent the best years of his youth in quacks' clinics and selling more pills than he could count. He bought heroin balloons in Cincinnati from Mexicans. He had two kids but didn't know what it was like to raise a child sober. He'd gone to prison and returned to Aberdeen.

To an outsider, Aberdeen looked to be the salt of America's earth, a place of farms and families. But the Aberdeen that Wilder knew was a sewer of pills and needles; the county had the highest rate of drug overdoses in Ohio.

He called a childhood friend living in Portsmouth. The friend was also an addict, but Wilder didn't know what else to do. He needed to get away. The guy said he didn't have much, just a couch in a small apartment, but Wilder was welcome to it.

Wilder left his cell phone in Aberdeen—every contact in it was an addict or a dealer. His father drove him to Portsmouth and gave him a little cash and those Percocets to tide him over.

"Good luck," his father said, and drove off.

This wasn't exactly the ideal spot. Wilder knew the town once had jobs, now had none, and instead teemed with dope fiends. The doctors who prescribed his pills learned the trade here. But with no other hope, he hugged Portsmouth like a life raft.

As it happened, Wilder wasn't the only one seeking rebirth in this beat-down town.

The bottom for Portsmouth came in 2009. The nation was in the throes of a once-in-a-generation financial crisis; a pill plague was consuming its children; and Mitchellace, the town's last shoe-industry factory, was about to close.

But as any addict knows, rock bottom is where recovery begins. That's what happened with Mitchellace. Then it happened in Portsmouth, too.

Nelson Smith, a local construction company owner, heard about the factory's bankruptcy and called Bryan Davis, the vice president of sales, who had worked at Mitchellace since he was a kid.

"This isn't going to happen," Smith said. "We're going to save these jobs." He asked Davis, "Are you on board?"

"Well," Davis said, "I don't have a whole lot else going on."

Smith assembled a group of local businessmen who put up their own money to keep the plant afloat. The team wrote a business plan and named their proposed company Sole Choice. Two weeks later, a judge picked their bid for the company over two others.

"It took individuals to say, 'No more,'" Davis said later, over the roar of bobbins spinning out streams of shoelaces.

Three floors of the plant were still empty. Davis saw that as room to grow. Sole Choice now had three hundred customers, up from twenty-four. Forty people had their jobs back and more were coming on. The company exported shoelaces to thirty countries, including China and Taiwan.

"It wasn't about the laces; it was about the people," said Davis, who is also a Republican Party leader in Scioto County. The real entrepreneurial spirit, he said, is about "people, relationships, about building communities." If you have that, he said, money will follow.

By the time Mitchellace was becoming Sole Choice, Scioto County coroner Terry Johnson had spent most of a decade raising hell about the mounting corpses from pill overdoses in and around Portsmouth—to little avail.

Doctors had failed people, he felt. "We visited incredible harm on the people of America as a profession," he said. "Pharmacists did also. Every single pill that was killing people in my county was legitimately prescribed, legitimately filled, legitimately paid for."

In 2010, Johnson was elected to Ohio's House of Representatives, the first Republican to hold the Portsmouth seat. After he took office, he and fellow representative Dave Burke, a pharmacist, wrote House Bill 93, which defined and regulated pain clinics. Their bill made it illegal, among other things, for a convicted felon to run one. Doctors could no longer dispense pharmaceuticals from their clinics—a widespread pill mill practice up to that point. It also called for repeal of the state's intractable pain law, which exempted doctors from prosecution when prescribing opiates under the law's more relaxed guidelines.

In a politically divided state, House Bill 93 passed unanimously in May 2011. Together, Ohio Republicans and Democrats repealed the state's intractable pain law.

The same week the bill passed, agents swarmed in and shut down a half dozen pain clinics in the largest drug raid in Scioto County history. The move ended the era of pill mills in Portsmouth. None have reopened.

Meanwhile, churches in town formed an alliance against the pill mills. Tom Rayburn, a member of the First Apostolic Church, was asked to come up with a plan. "The Lord said, 'Have seven marches,'" Rayburn told me. "Seven is God's number."

Marches went by two notorious housing projects and around the jail and through downtown. One march circled a pill mill seven times. Protestors stopped at the clinic door. A nurse came out. They were blocking traffic, she yelled. The marchers started singing "Amazing Grace." A local pastor pulled out a shofar—a ram's horn like the one Joshua used at Jericho—and blew.

Shortly after House Bill 93 passed, the seventh march was to wind through East Portsmouth, a poor neighborhood wedged between the railroad tracks and the Ohio River. That afternoon felt ominous. The dark skies delivered a cold rain on the one hundred marchers as they snaked through the East End.

But as the march ended, the torrents ceased. As marchers shivered and began to dry, a rainbow arced over the massive Mitchellace factory. The skies cleared. The sun came out and a strange light, cleansing rain fell. As it did, another rainbow appeared, crossing the first in the sky. People stopped and gazed up at the double rainbow embracing Portsmouth from the East End to the west.

"People were coming out of their doors," said Lisa Roberts, the city's public health nurse. "It got real bright. We had been a town in constant mourning. Every week there was another death. Now the flood was over, this flood of pills. It was like receiving visions of the Virgin Mary or something. It was as if this devil, this evil was lifted."

The scourge was not completely gone, however. Without pill mills, many in the town's oversized population of opiate addicts switched to heroin. Crime went up. Detroit dealers of powder heroin began flowing down through Portsmouth. Addicts began going to Columbus for cheap black tar. Before long, you could get either powder or tar heroin in the town where Dreamland once stood.

Pills remained a problem as well. In the last year of the pill mills, 9.7 million pills were legally prescribed in the county of eighty thousand people. Two years later, 7 million pills were still prescribed there annually.

Nevertheless, closing the cynical clinics was a necessary beginning. Like the rescue of Mitchellace, it was an action townspeople took to determine their own future, instead of letting it happen to them.

That became a theme of sorts.

Scott Douthat, a sociology professor at Shawnee State University in Portsmouth, had a class study the town's problems and propose solutions that required no extra budget. The students urged the city to apply for a federal Community Oriented Policing Grant, which it won. Now there were more officers on the streets. Buy a floodlight for a beleaguered downtown park, the students suggested. Prostitutes magically moved elsewhere.

The students suggested including litter pickup as part of each probationer's sentence and volunteered to help a judge organize the program because the city didn't have money for staff. Probationers picked up ninety tons of litter in the first three months.

This was all Municipal Governance 101, but it seemed radically refreshing to a town emerging from a thirty-year narco-economic fog. Residents, meanwhile, realized that the city had almost no budget. Churches, Boy Scouts, and other groups began regular civic cleanups at parks and along the river.

Several buildings downtown were under renovation. A Cincinnati clothing storeowner named Terry Ockerman moved back to Scioto County, where he grew up. Ockerman bought an empty four-story furniture store downtown and renovated it into gleaming, modern lofts. He had a waiting list to rent them. Next door, he was putting in a café with outdoor tables, a place where people could actually meet and converse.

"Loft living and cafés—what's hipper than that?" he said.

Far more vital was the kind of stuff a young guy named Clint Askew was creating. Askew had assembled a clan of nine or ten friends obsessed with rap music. Late at night, at his job as a market clerk, he began working out raps and choruses and beats to go with them. His friends added lyrics of their own. Raw Word Revival was born.

Askew had grown up in Portsmouth and took the town as his raw material, shaping rhymes, like a journalist, from what was around him. He had never used pills but watched many of his generation die or walk the streets in tatters looking for a fix.

One night at the market where he worked, a hook occurred to him.

What did people really know about this forgotten place? He fastened on its area code, 740, and came up with a chorus:

What the hell you know about the 7-4-0?
If you ain't lived here, worked here, sold here
If you ain't caught a case here.
What the hell you know about this place here?

Others in RWR added raps, telling what they knew of growing up here. The song was a cry from out of the Walmart world of rural heartland America, white Appalachian rap about American decline and rebirth.

Used to be known as the 6-1-4
Now it's just known for the devil at your door
Pain clinics, pill mills
Factories, drug deals . . .
Yes I'm aware an' I care
An' I'm ready to revive our greatness
But be patient
'Cause a big black cloud's hang'n over our town
Flash flood a lotta people going my route wound
Up gettin' drowned . . .

They filmed a video on an iPhone at locations around town. Thousands of people watched it on Facebook. The track boomed from cars, people sang it in Walmart. People who hated rap loved the song. Portsmouth suddenly had some rousing, truth-telling art to rally around.

It didn't take long for folks to see the 740 elsewhere. The 740 was in Floyd County, Kentucky, and in Marion, Ohio. It was in Chimayo, New Mexico, and in the meatpacking towns in southwest Kansas. It was in those long, dreary lines outside the offices of David Procter, down any Walmart aisle, and in that parking lot where Dreamland once stood.

The most remarkable sign of change in the town was that slowly, hundreds of addicts were turning away from dope. Close to 10 percent of the town was in recovery. Portsmouth led the country into the opiate epidemic and was now poised to lead it out as well.

Hard-held attitudes in conservative Scioto County softened. Recovering addicts now had an easier time finding work. Everyone had friends or family on dope. Some employers believed in second chances. Others saw little choice. Those who were in recovery were at least going to pass a drug test. Even if many people relapsed after finding work, it was a start.

Getting clean awoke a creativity and imagination in those who made it back. Addicts in recovery were infusing Portsmouth with what other American cities relied on immigrants to provide: energy, optimism, gratitude for an opportunity.

Portsmouth's resurrection was sprouting from the rubble of the town's decline. The town was positioned to be a national center for addiction research and treatment. It had thousands of addicts—both active and recovering—and lots of vacant buildings to expand into.

"Now we're being looked at as leaders because we have the experience and we know how this works," Lisa Roberts said as the recovery took root.

Indeed, Scioto County was ahead of the country in a lot of ways. As fatal overdoses set records in the state and the nation, they fell in Scioto County. The county had a needle exchange program that took in a hundred thousand syringes a year; new hepatitis C cases dropped by half. Addicts saved twenty-three people from overdosing with naloxone they were given through a state-funded pilot project.

Twelve-step meetings were all over town, sometimes several a day. Addicts saw examples all around them of people getting clean and happy. A newly recovering addict now had mentors to call at three a.m. who knew how hard things could get. Many recovering addicts had applied to Shawnee State, hoping to become social workers or drug counselors. The school was adding professors, a bachelor's of social work, and a psychology master's degree, all with a focus on addiction.

The Counseling Center had doubled in size during the epidemic. It now occupied some of Portsmouth's many abandoned buildings and provided jobs to two hundred people, most of whom were in recovery and had criminal records.

The Counseling Center employed Jarrett Withrow, who'd been part of that ironworking crew that went to Florida and found a pill haven. Kathy Newman, who'd gone to David Procter for help with pain from her car accident, was now clean and working there, too. Addicts intent on recovery could now have fun without drinking or using dope. The Counseling Center opened the Clubhouse, the largest drug-free hangout of its kind in Ohio. It held dances and card games and 12-step meetings.

Managing the Clubhouse, of all people, was Mary Ann Henson. Mary Ann, facing felony charges, had finally gotten clean in 2010. Her husband, Keith Henson, had stopped using, too. Their son, Luke, was eight, and with two sober parents, he was a happy kid.

Angie Thuma, the veteran Walmart shoplifter, was hoping one day for a job at the Counseling Center. She was twenty months clean and working as a cashier for minimum wage, earning $230 a week and supporting her two sons while living with her parents. Shoplifting charges got her banned from Walmart, so shopping now was a chore. And she wasn't going to apply for the assistant manager's job where she worked, fearing a background check would reveal her past.

Yet, she said, "When I think about all the things I went through and I'm still alive, it gives you courage to keep bettering yourself."

That seemed to be Portsmouth's attitude. The town still looked as scarred and beaten as an addict's arm. Too many jobs paid minimum wage and led nowhere. Portsmouth still had hundreds of drug addicts and dealers. But it also now had a confident, muscular culture of recovery that competed with the culture of getting high.

Proof of that was that addicts from all over Ohio were now migrating south to get *clean* in Portsmouth. Even David Procter's mansion across the river was converted into a rehab facility. No other place in Ohio had the town's recovery infrastructure.

Once a junkie's haven, it was now a refuge for those seeking a new life. A young woman from Johnstown, a rural town northeast of Columbus, had been buying heroin from the Xalisco Boys in Columbus for a couple of years. When she tried to quit, a driver who spoke English called her for a week straight.

"But, señorita, we have really good stuff. It just came in."

Finally, she threw away her phone. There wasn't much on it but dope contacts anyway. She was twenty-three, alone with a ten-month-old son, and—seeking to get clean with nowhere else to turn—she went to Portsmouth.

"I love it here. I'm really afraid to go back," she said.

So the battered old town had hung on. It was, somehow, a beacon embracing shivering and hollow-eyed addicts, letting them know that all was not lost. That at the bottom of the rubble was a place just like them, kicked and battered but surviving. A place that had, like them, shredded and lost so much that was precious but was nurturing it again. Though they were adrift, they, too, could begin to find their way back.

Back to that place called Dreamland.

PHOTO
ALBUM

Matt Schoonover as a high school baseball player.

Postcard of the Dreamland pool.

The Ohio River running through Portsmouth.

Dr. David Procter's mansion, later converted to a
drug rehabilitation clinic.

Tyler Campbell (left) tackling during the first football game of his sophomore year.

A wall at the Portsmouth SOLACE headquarters commemorating victims of the opiate epidemic.

Training notes from Purdue Pharma sales representatives, as shown in court documents.

Kathy Newman, a former OxyContin user, holding her son.

DISCUSSION GUIDE

The following questions are intended to enhance your discussion of *Dreamland*.

1. Consider the title *Dreamland*. What does it refer to? How does it work as a symbol to explain the themes of this book?
2. What are the typical preconceived notions that a reader might have about opiate addiction? In what ways does the book work against those ideas?
3. Explain the connection between OxyContin and black tar heroin. How are they similar? How are they different? How does the existence of both forms of opiates feed into addiction?
4. Discuss Purdue Pharma's marketing of OxyContin. Do companies like Purdue have a responsibility to be more transparent with their consumers? Why or why not?
5. Why are teens particularly susceptible to opiate addiction?
6. How have medical practitioners contributed to the rise of opiate addiction? Do you think that any of the doctors and researchers in this book were justified in their reasoning and methods?
7. The concept of rehabilitation comes up in the book as some of the characters try to get clean. What versions of rehabilitation seem effective? How can systems be put into place to give addicts more help?
8. The book discusses law enforcement and criminal justice. In what

ways have police forces and the courts been successful in dealing with addiction? In what ways can they improve and use better strategies to help addicts?

9. According to their interviews, the Xalisco Boys rarely sell to African Americans. Why is this? How do race relations play into the ways that opiates are distributed and used? Do race relations affect how opiate addiction is perceived in comparison to other drug addictions?

RESOURCES FOR TEENS

If you or someone in your family is struggling with addiction, you can visit these websites to find help.

211
    www.211.org
Alateen
    https://al-anon.org/for-members/group-resources/alateen/
Center on Addiction and Partnership for Drug-Free Kids
    https://www.centeronaddiction.org/
National Council on Alcoholism and Drug Dependence
    https://www.ncadd.org/
National Institute on Drug Abuse for Teens
    https://teens.drugabuse.gov/
Substance Abuse and Mental Health Services Administration
    (SAMHSA)
    https://www.samhsa.gov/
TeenLink
    https://866teenlink.org/

You can also reach out to a guidance counselor, teacher, or other trusted adult.

SOURCES

This book was written based primarily on interviews I did over a five-year period but especially in 2009 as a reporter for the *Los Angeles Times* and from 2012 to 2014.

While I was at the *Times,* I was part of a team covering Mexico's drug wars. My job was to write about Mexican trafficking in the United States. Searching for a story to do, I had come upon reports of a 2007 black tar heroin outbreak in Huntington, West Virginia, and called a Huntington police narcotics sergeant.

All our black tar heroin comes from Columbus, Ohio, he told me.

I called the DEA in Columbus and spoke with an especially talkative agent.

"We got dozens of Mexican heroin traffickers. They all drive around selling their dope in small balloons, delivering it to the addicts. They're like teams, or cells. We arrest the drivers all the time and they send new ones up from Mexico," he said. "They never go away."

They hide among Columbus's large Mexican population, he said. The drivers all know each other and never talk. They're never armed. They come, give false names, rent apartments, and are gone six months later.

"Crazy thing," he said. "They're all from the same town."

I sat up in my chair. "Yeah, which one's that?"

He called over a colleague. They talked in muted tones for a couple of minutes.

The DEA agent came back to the phone. "Tepic," he said.

No, that's wrong, I thought. Tepic is the capital of one of Mexico's smallest states—Nayarit, on the Pacific coast. But it's still a big city, population 330,000.

My hunch was that the family and personal connections crucial to the system he was describing would only be forged in a small town or rancho, wild, lawless places on the outskirts of civilization. During the ten years I lived in Mexico as a freelance writer, I spent a lot of time writing about people who migrated north, as well as two books of nonfiction stories about Mexico. Many of the stories took place in the ranchos.

By the time I got off the phone, that prospect had me mesmerized. I imagined some rancho of heroin traffickers expert enough to supply a town the size of Columbus. People from the Mexican rancho had become a huge influence in American life. It gave rise to millions of our new working class. Mexican immigrant customs and attitudes toward work, sex, politics, civic engagement, government, education, debt, leisure—they were forged in the rancho.

I wrote to a dozen of the drivers arrested in Columbus who were doing time in federal prisons, asking if they wanted to talk to a reporter. Weeks passed. I was about to turn to other stories when one of them called collect. He'd worked, and was arrested, in Columbus. He was now doing many years in prison. He had lots of information. Most startling: Columbus was not the only town they worked, he told me.

"They're in many others. All over the country," he said. Salt Lake, Charlotte, Las Vegas, Cincinnati, Nashville, Minneapolis, Columbia, Indianapolis, Honolulu. The cities he mentioned all had large white middle classes that benefited hugely from the economic booms of the previous dozen years and now had large Mexican immigrant populations as well.

Were there heroin markets in these towns? I wondered. Yes, he assured me, they were big and getting bigger. He hadn't even mentioned America's traditional heroin capital, I noticed.

"No, in New York are gangs, with guns," he said. "They're afraid of New York City. They don't go to New York."

Mexican traffickers afraid of gangs and gunplay? From one tiny town? Selling tar heroin in not just Columbus, but as much as half the United States, including now a bunch of cities east of the Mississippi River for the first time?

Right there, I was hooked.

Cops say they're from Tepic, I said finally.

"No, they're not from Tepic," he said. "That's what they say, but they're not."

From that conversation, I was on my way.

To tell this story, I interviewed parents of addicts in several states, and many addicts themselves, public health nurses and epidemiologists, defense attorneys, doctors, local cops, drug rehabilitation counselors and administrators, pain specialists, chemists, a pain historian, state and federal prosecutors, DEA and FBI agents, as well as more than a dozen Xalisco Boys, most of whom were in prison at the time.

The fellow I call the Man I interviewed eight or ten times, in person and over the telephone. Much of what he said I knew to be true or found ways of confirming. His knowledge of Xalisco was detailed; so, too, was his knowledge of methadone clinics in cities of America. Later, I spoke with a DEA agent who had worked on Operation Tar Pit. He confirmed the Man's role, which he knew from listening to endless hours of wiretaps.

I traveled widely to get those interviews. Several times I visited Columbus and Portsmouth, Ohio, and went to Marion twice and Cincinnati once. As the research proceeded, I found myself three times in both Portland, Oregon, and Denver. I went to Indianapolis and Nashville; to northern and eastern Kentucky; to Charlotte, North Carolina; Boise, Idaho; Phoenix, Arizona; Huntington, West Virginia; and Albuquerque and Chimayo, New Mexico.

Part of my research involved a trip to Xalisco for four days during the Feria del Elote while I was employed at the *Los Angeles Times*, from which I wrote a three-part series on the town and its pizza-delivery model for retailing heroin. That trip remains the only time in my career when I've lied when asked what I did for a living. I told people who asked that a photographer colleague and I were tourists, Spanish teachers in California. At this point in Mexico, beheadings and mass slaughter were the order of the day. Bodies were hung from overpasses and left in piles on street corners. Many reporters were murdered. Against that context, I hope the journalism gods will forgive my trespass in Xalisco. We left the town when, in an encounter that seemed far too coincidental, I was introduced to a man I was told was the Nayarit state police supervisor of the antikidnapping squad, who watched me far too closely while I watched a basketball game during the fair. I spoke with numerous traffickers, drivers, telephone operators, and suppliers from Xalisco. Most would speak only of what they did, and would not discuss the activities of others. This was especially true of the man known as Enrique. Most of these people I tried to know only by first names, for their protection and for my own.

A trial transcript is a great friend to a crime reporter. But because

Xalisco Boys almost always plead guilty to their cases, I had very few trial transcripts available in piecing together their story. One important and early one, though, was a large case against Luis Padilla-Peña in Omaha, Nebraska. That case came just as the Boys were beginning their expansion out of the San Fernando Valley. I'm indebted to prosecutor William Mickle for his help in procuring that very long transcript.

Indictments against the Xalisco Boys, on the other hand, are plentiful and helpful for two reasons, mainly. Though they were not intimately detailed, the indictments did tell the same story over and over. They resembled one another so much that reading indictments from Charlotte to Portland to Phoenix and points in between gave me confidence early on in my research that this system was being faithfully duplicated across America. Also, indictments gave me names—of prosecutors and sometimes investigators with whom I later spoke, and of Xalisco defendants, by then in prison, to whom I wrote requesting interviews.

Another invaluable transcript, by the way, was from the trial against Michael Leman, owner of the Urgent Care Services clinics in Slidell, Louisiana; Philadelphia; and Cincinnati. Along with interviews, they provided a fascinating view of how the pill problem exploded in one eastern Kentucky county—Floyd. I added to that with interviews with local prosecutor Brent Turner and his father, Arnold Turner, a former prosecutor; with Randy Hunter, a recently retired state police detective; and with a prison interview with Timmy Wayne Hall, one of the biggest pill dealers in Floyd County.

Most of my research into Portsmouth, Ohio, came from interviews with residents on visits I made to the town, as well as a Facebook page devoted to the town's diaspora and how Portsmouth used to be. Much of my information about Dreamland came from people on that page. There were occasional news and historical journal articles as well that filled in parts of the story of the town's decline and the history of that fabulous pool.

Information on David Procter and his physician progeny I obtained from, first, interviews with people in Portsmouth. I also relied on reports from Kentucky's Board of Medical Licensure for Procter as well as several of the doctors who had worked for him. Newspaper articles about those doctors and other pill mill owners who came later were also invaluable.

Several books informed my sections on opium, morphine, heroin, the Harrison Act, and the Narcotic Farm. Martin Booth's *Opium: A History* is the classic history of the poppy and the goo it produces that has been so much a part of human history. Other books that I turned to were:

The American Disease: Origins of Narcotic Control, David F. Musto (Oxford University Press, 3rd edition, 1999).

Creating the American Junkie: Addiction Research in the Classic Era of Narcotic Control, Caroline Jean Acker (Johns Hopkins University Press, 2005).

Dark Paradise: A History of Opiate Addiction in America, David Courtwright (Harvard University Press; enlarged edition, 2001).

Junky: The Definitive Text of "Junk" (50th Anniversary edition), William S. Burroughs (Grove Press, 2003).

The Narcotic Farm: The Rise and Fall of America's First Prison for Drug Addicts, Nancy Campbell, J. P. Olsen, and Luke Walden (Abrams, 2008).

One Hundred Years of Heroin, ed. David F. Musto (Praeger, 2002).

Opioids and Pain Relief: A Historical Perspective, ed. Marcia L. Meldrum (IASP Press, 2003).

Smack: Heroin and the American City, Eric C. Schneider (University of Pennsylvania Press, 2008).

Wellcome Witnesses to Twentieth Century Medicine, Volume 21: Innovation in Pain Management, ed. L. A. Reynolds and E. M. Tansey (QMUL History C20 Medicine, 2004).

For the sections on the revolution in pain treatment, I relied on recollections from doctors who were practicing or in residency in the late 1980s and early 1990s. *Innovation in Pain Management* provided essential details on the early approaches to pain management, into Cicely Saunders and Robert Twycross at St. Christopher's in England, and into Jan Stjernsward's development of the WHO Ladder. I also relied on oral histories that Professor Marcia Meldrum did with Kathleen Foley and Russell Portenoy, which are available at the John C. Liebeskind History of Pain Collection at UCLA.

To chronicle the spread of the abuse of opiates I relied on studies by several government agencies, primarily Substance Abuse and Mental Health Services Administration and the Centers for Disease Control. The GAO, now renamed the US Government Accountability Office, produced two important reports. One was a report analyzing the state of methadone clinics in America. The other was a 2003 analysis of Purdue Pharma's promotion campaign for the first half dozen years after releasing OxyContin.

To describe Purdue's campaign, I also used interviews with doctors, including the late Phillip Prior, news articles, advertisements from medical journals, parts of Barry Meier's book *Pain Killer*, and an interview with former US attorney John Brownlee.

Through this odyssey, I relied also on my experience over twenty-seven years as a journalist. I learned reporting covering crime for four years in the great town of Stockton, California. In my decade living in and traveling across Mexico, I had a chance to tell much longer stories. I reveled in the sagas of ranchos, *valientes*, *corridos*, *pistoleros*, and in the novel that each immigrant life comprises. You can read more about that in my two previous books: *True Tales from Another Mexico: The Lynch Mob, the Popsicle Kings, Chalino, and the Bronx* and *Antonio's Gun and Delfino's Dream: True Tales of Mexican Migration*.

Finally, I invite you to visit my website, www.samquinones.com. There I've listed, and linked to, many more resources—including recorded audio and video interviews and several relevant music videos on YouTube—that I used to tell this true tale.

PHOTOGRAPH CREDITS

Courtesy of the Schoonover family: 191; courtesy of the Portsmouth Public Library: 192, top; Joel Prince/*The Washington Post*/Getty Images: 192, bottom; 194, top; 194, bottom; courtesy of the author: 193, top; AP Images/Andy Manis: 193, bottom; courtesy of Circuit Court of Knox County Court Records: 194, center.

INDEX

Note: Page numbers in italics indicate illustrations.

Aberdeen, Ohio, 86–87, 180–181
Aberrant use behavior, 169
Abingdon, Virginia, 122–129, 170
Abuse-deterrent formulation, 128–129, 169–170
Accreditation Council for Continuing Medical Education, 124
Activism, 156–165; addictsmom.com, 168–169; Chimayo protests, 93; Portsmouth recovery and rebirth, 181–190; Schoonovers and, 163–165; SOLACE, 157–158, *194*; Tyler's Light, 162–163
Addiction: adolescent, 103–108; combining opiates with benzodiazepine and, 9, 31, 134; confronting epidemic of, 166–173; cost of maintaining heroin habit, 74; crime (thefts) related to, 35–39; discovery of crisis, 42–47; firsthand exposure to, impact of, 152–155; legal protection of doctors in, 18, 135; methadone maintenance for, 78–79; openness and activism about, 156–165; opiate-blocking drug for, 172; OxyContin, 20–26; Portsmouth as center of study of, 187; Procter's prescribing practices and, 9–12, 28; research on, misinterpretation and misuse of, 125–126; Schoonover (Matt) and, 1–4, 163–165; silence and shame about, 136–140, 157, 162; sports injuries and, 158–162; study of, separated from pain research, 170–171
Addicts: athletes as, 158–162; crimes (thefts) committed by, 35–40; as dope fiends, 56; drug courts and softening approach to, 151–155, 177–178; drug-seeking behavior of, 25; "fifteen-year-old brain" of, 164; as guides for Xalisco Boys, 77–80; legends among Xalisco Boys, 80; OxyContin and creation of, 27, 86–87; privately insured, 138; recovering, in Portsmouth, 187–189; as street rats, 37; targeted at methadone clinics, 78–80; women, preying upon, 115–116
addictsmom.com, 168–169
African Americans: hardline approach for, 151, 154–155; Xalisco Boys' refusal to deal with, 70
Age, of OxyContin abuser, 105
Akron, Ohio, 24–25, 159–162
Albuquerque, New Mexico: author's research in, 201; DEA base in, 93; Enrique in, 66, 91, 99; increase in heroin use, 167; participation in Operation Tar Pit, 96, 99; Xalisco Boys operations in, 66, 115

American Academy of Pediatrics, 108
American Pain Society, 17–18
"Angel" (McLachlan song), 157
Arrests and prosecution: author's use of trial transcripts, 201–202; Charlotte policy, 138–139; Chimayo investigation, 95; criminal case against Purdue Pharma, 45–47, 122–129; drug courts/ treatment *versus* hardline approach, 151–155, 177–178; Enrique, 99; information from indictments, 202; Len Bias cases, 143–148; The Man, 100; minimal impact of, 100, 121, 139; Operation Black Gold Rush, 116, 119–121, 175; Operation Tar Pit, 96–100, 117, 178–179, 200–201; as opportunity for change, 178–179; Procter and associated doctors, 31; Xalisco Boys' rebound after, 100, 121, 139
Ashland, Kentucky, 84
Askew, Clint, 185–187
Athletes: exceptions made for, 156, 158–159; opiates prescribed for injuries in, 158–162; as trendsetters for drug use, 158–159; University of Akron football team, 159–162
Atlanta, Georgia, 117, 154
Avocado industry, 176

Baker, Connie, 18
Balloons, heroin-filled, 55, 57, 68–69, 114–115; chipmunk appearance of drivers, 68; deals and enticements, 70, 114; price in Charlotte, 139; price in Columbus, 85; spitting out when paid, 69; swallowing, 68
Baltimore, Maryland, 88, 116
Barela family, 94
Bayer Laboratory, 55
Beeghly, Christy, 133–134, 136–137
Bend, Oregon, 147
Benzodiazepines, 9, 31, 134, 166
Berardinelli, Robert, 178–179
Bernal family, 61
Bias, Len, 143–144
Bickers, Kathleen, 147
Billings, Montana, 95
Black tar heroin, 56–57; in Albuquerque, 66, 91, 93, 96, 99, 115, 167, 201; in Boise, 72–73, 95, 201; changes and challenges in trade, 174–179; in Charlotte, 89, 138–140, 175; clans and

INDEX

Importing pills, 109–113; bootlegging culture and, 110–111; from Florida, 109–110, 113; OxyContin Express, 113; restrictions prompting, 109; from Urgent Care Services, 111–112, 202
Impulsivity of addicts, 164
Indiana, Nashville connections with, 120
Indianapolis, Indiana, 81, 175, 199, 201
InfoCision Stadium, 160
Injecting: heroin, 56; "muscling," 56–57; OxyContin, 24, 124, 128–129, 169–170
Innovation in Pain Management (Reynolds and Tansey eds.), 204
Insurance companies: costs and quick-fix pressures, 16–17; privately insured addicts, 138; resistance to multidisciplinary care, 171; resistance to treating teenage addicts, 108
Intractable pain regulations, 18, 135, 182–183
Ironton, Ohio, 158

Jacksonville, Florida, 88
Jacquemain, Chris, 160
Jaime (undercover officer), 138–140
Jeans: exchange rate for heroin, 71; as status symbol, 54–55, 58, 64, 71–72
Jefferson, Tracy, 80
Jick, Herschel, 125–126
Johnson, Terry, 134, 182–183
Johnstown, Ohio, 189
Joint Commission for the Accreditation of Healthcare Organizations, 171

Kasich, John, 153, 172
Kentucky: author's research in, 201; bootlegging culture of, 110–111; drug courts in, 153–154; as ground zero for opiate epidemic, 105; importing pills into, 109–113, 202; Nashville connections with, 120; OxyContin overdose deaths in, 46; OxyContin spread into, 32; prescription monitoring system of, 109; Procter's operations in, 8, 10, 25, 28–29; Procter's prosecution in, 31; Procter's proteges and pill mills in, 29–31; proximity to Columbus heroin trade, 83–84. *See also specific locations*
Kentucky Board of Medical Licensure, investigation of Procter, 10, 28–29, 203
Klimusko, Austin, 168
Klimusko, Susan, 168
Knox, Cecil, 46
Krohn, Jo Anna, 156–158
Kuykendall, Jim, 93–95, 96, 99, 178–179

Lancaster, Ohio, 106
Landarenas (Xalisco neighborhood), 176
Langarica, Chuy, 61
Langarica, Julio, 61
Langarica, Tino, 61
Las Vegas, Nevada, 78, 119, 199
Law enforcement. *See* Drug Enforcement Administration; Police
Leman, Michael, 111, 202
Len Bias cases, 143–148

Levi's 501s: exchange rate for heroin, 71; as status symbol, 54–55, 58, 64, 71–72
Lilly, John, 33–34
Lockhart, Jerry, 37
Loeser, John, 16–17
Lopez, Marina, 96–99
Lorcet, 23, 30, 34, 111
Lorentz, Chuck, 8
Lortab, 15, 23, 28, 30, 124
Los Angeles: heroin supply from, 85, 96–97; lure of Enrique's family in, 52
Los Angeles Times, 198, 201
Los Hermanos Penitentes, 93
Louisiana, importing pills from, 111, 202

Mabry, Dennis, 120
Mafia, markets sought without influence of, 78, 83, 88
Mai, Jaymie, 42–45, 47, 130–132, 135
The Man, 75–89; arrest and imprisonment of, 100; author's interviews with, 200–201; Columbus operations of, 83–89, 106; Columbus targeted by, 77, 82; police encounter in Indianapolis, 81; prison time with Xalisco Boy, 75; as self-described drug merchant, 75; time spent in Nayarit, 76–77, 80–81; toll of time on, 176–177; wiretapped conversations of, 96–97
Mario (dispatcher), 117–118
Marion County, Ohio, 172
Marshall, Donnie R., 99
Martin, Bob, 138
Martinez, Jess "Donuts," 94–95
Martinez clan, 94
Maui, Hawaii, 99
McLachlan, Sarah, 157
Mecklenburg County, North Carolina, 138–140. *See also* Charlotte, North Carolina
Medicaid: expansion in Ohio, 172; and obtaining OxyContin, 34–35
Medication use disorders, 169
Meier, Barry, 205
Meldrum, Marcia, 204
Memphis, Tennessee, 78, 119, 175
Methadone, 78–79, 113
Methadone clinics: in Columbus, 82, 84; in Simi Valley, 168; as target for The Man, 81, 82, 84, 89; as target for Xalisco Boys, 78–80
Mexican immigrants: in Columbus, 83; deportation of, 90–91; Operation Tar Pit discoveries about, 99–100; targeting towns with large populations of, 78, 199–200
Michocán, Mexico, 176
Mickle, William, 202
Miller, Jennifer, 172
Milwaukie, Oregon, 144, 147
Minneapolis, Minnesota, 199
Misbranding, Purdue Pharma's guilty plea for, 127–129
Mitchellace factory (Portsmouth, Ohio), 181–182, 183, 184
Mohr, Gary, 153

211

INDEX

Valium, 9, 29, 31
Van Nuys, California, 75
VanDerKarr, Scott, 177–178
Vermont, heroin in, 167
Veterans Health Administration, 18, 171
Vicious, Sid, 106
Vicodin: abuse and street trade of, 23; abuse
   potential of OxyContin *versus,* 124; athletes
   receiving for sports injuries, 159; changing
   approach to prescribing, 15, 105; FDA
   reclassification of, 170; Procter's prescription of,
   10–11, 29; spread of pill mills, 109–110
Virginia: Brownlee's investigation, 45–47, 122–129,
   170; The Man's scouting in, 88
Vital sign, pain as, 18, 171
Vivitrol, 172

Wake-up call, need for, 136–140
Wall Street Journal, 153
Walmart: refunds and gift cards from, 40;
   shoplifting from, 38–40, 188–189
Warning label, for OxyContin, 21, 24
Washington Post, 127–128
Washington State: decline in overdose deaths, 169;
   Department of Labor and Industries investigation,
   42–45, 47, 130–132; prescribing guidelines in,
   131–132, 135, 169. *See also specific locations*
Websites, funded by Purdue Pharma, 23
West, Gavin, 171
West Virginia: as ground zero for opiate epidemic,
   105; heroin overdose deaths in, 167; importing
   pills into, 113; The Man's expansion into,
   85–88; OxyContin overdose deaths in, 46;
   OxyContin spread into, 32; OxyContin-seeking
   travelers from, 113; proximity to Columbus
   heroin trade, 83–84, 198; Purdue Pharma sales
   in, 23. *See also specific locations*
Wheeling, West Virginia, 83, 85–88, 97
Whites: as preferred target of drug dealers, 70, 82, 118;
   treatment *versus* punishment for, 151, 154–155
Whitney, Richard, 164
WHO Ladder, 15–16, 19, 204
Wilder, Jeremy, 83–84, 180–181
Williams, Fortune, 30, 31
Wiretaps, Operation Tar Pit, 96–100
Withdrawal: morphine (opiate), 14–15;
   OxyContin, 123; treating teenage heroin
   addicts, 103–105, 107–108
Withrow, Jarrett, 109–110, 188
Women addicts, preying upon, 115–116
Wong, Donna, 18
Workers' compensation, 28, 42–45
Workman, Wes, 156–158
World Health Organization, 15–16, 204
Wright, Curtis, 21

Xalisco, Nayarit: author's research trip to, 201;
   avocado industry in, 176; cartel violence in,
   174–175; construction boom in, 71; Corn
   Festival in, 65, 72, 88, 100, 174, 201; dream
   of returning to, 71; The Man's visits and life in,
   76–77, 80–81; money sent home to, 64, 71, 84;
   in Nashville, 117–121; Operation Tar Pit impact
   on, 100; outcomes of heroin trade in, 174–177;
   pronunciation and spelling of, 68; rank among
   wealthiest counties, 174; recruitment of drivers
   outside families, 117–118; sugarcane farmers
   in, 4, 51–53, 62–63; US prison *versus* living in,
   118–119
Xalisco Boys: addicts as guides for, 77–80;
   in Albuquerque, 66, 115; author's
   discoveries and investigation, 198–200;
   avoidance of gangs and Mafia, 78, 83, 88,
   116–117; in Boise, 72–73, 95, 201; boom-or-
   bust cycle for, 176; cell managers, 68; changes
   and challenges for, 174–179; in Charlotte, 89,
   138–140, 175; in Chimayo, 92–95; clans and
   families, 61; in Columbus, 83–89, 103–108,
   117–118, 175, 198–200; competition among,
   60, 69, 72–73, 88–89, 100; competition
   from other Mexican traffickers, 116–117;
   delivery model and cell operations of, 68–70,
   97, 114–115; in Denver, 67–72, 76, 95;
   dispatcher, 117–118; drivers, 68–70, 114–119
   (*See also* Drivers, Xalisco Boys); Enrique,
   51–66, 90–92, 99; expanding markets of,
   62, 72, 106, 116–117, 175; homecomings
   of, 72; as internet of dope, 100; Len Bias
   cases against, 143–148; Levi's 501s as status
   symbol for, 54–55, 58, 64, 71–72; The Man
   and, 75–89; methadone clinics as targets of,
   78–80; national scope of, 97, 120; number of
   cells in mid-1990s, 70; Operation Black Gold
   Rush against, 116, 119–121, 175; Operation
   Tar Pit against, 96–100, 117, 178–179,
   200–201; OxyContin and marketing strategy
   of, 114, 119–120; in Phoenix, 63–66, 76,
   85; in Portland, 66, 73–74, 76, 79–80, 85,
   143–148; prejudice/racism of, 70; profit per
   kilo, 74; protection money to drug cartels,
   175; reconstitution after busts, 100, 121, 139;
   Russian Pentecostals and, 144–146; sales per
   day and per year, 69; in San Fernando Valley,
   54–55, 57–61, 119; small-trade preference
   of, 70; teenagers buying from, 103–108;
   telephone operators, 68–69; women addicts
   preyed upon by, 115–116
Xanax, 9, 28, 29, 30, 31, 34

Zanesville, Ohio, 84
Zohydro, 170

216